Breaking Free From Domestic Violence

A Survival Guide to Reclaiming Your Life and Freedom

Shannon Savoy

Published by Kellie Kelly World Publishing ®

All Scripture quotations, unless otherwise indicated, are taken from the New King James Version, Copyright 2022 by Thomas Nelson, Inc. Used by permission. All rights reserved.

Cover Design by Kellie Kelly World Media ®

Edited by Kellie Kelly World Publishing ®

Connect With Us on Instagram: @KellieKellyWorld

This book was authored under the guidance and expertise of Kellie Kelly World Publishing, who provided expert editorial guidance and creative direction throughout the process.

Dedication

To the Holy Spirit—Your guidance and unshakable protection were my lifeline when I was ensnared in domestic violence through a tormenting marriage with a narcissistic sociopath. Through Your infinite love and miraculous intervention, You led me to safety, lighting the way when the path seemed impossible. It is Your grace that gave me the strength to break free, and now, it is Your inspiration that moves me to help others find their way out of darkness.

To my beloved husband, Solomon—your steadfast love has been an anchor upon me as I rebuilt my life. Your presence in my journey is a testament to God's enduring grace and a beacon of hope in my world.

And to my precious children, Amari and Jadon—may you always remember your inherent worth and walk in the brilliance of the freedom and light that God has planned for you. You are my greatest joy and treasure.

To Chain Breakers—The courageous souls who have come together to support and uplift each other in the journey of overcoming narcissistic abuse. Your strength, empathy, and unwavering support from the heart of this community. Each story shared, each hand extended, and each moment of solidarity reflects the boundless power of collective healing.

May this guide be a testament to your resilience and a beacon of hope for all those seeking a way out of the shadows. Together, we break the chains and reclaim the light, one step at a time.

Disclaimer

While this book addresses the topic of domestic violence and includes discussions on definitions, dynamics, and relevant laws, it is not intended to serve as legal, medical, or professional advice. The information provided is for educational and informational purposes only. Readers are encouraged to seek guidance from qualified professionals, such as legal experts, counselors, or healthcare providers, for any specific concerns or situations related to domestic violence. The author and publisher are not responsible for any actions taken based on the content of this book.

Table of Contents

Introduction:
A Message of Hope

To the Brave Survivor,

As I sit down to write these words, my heart is heavy with empathy and overflowing with hope. **You are about to embark on a profound journey—a journey from darkness into light, from pain into healing.** This book is not just a collection of strategies and advice; it is a heartfelt message to you, a beacon of hope and strength for those who have endured the unimaginable.

If you are reading these words, you have already shown extraordinary courage. The path you have walked has been grueling and fraught with unimaginable challenges. **You have faced the storm, and now, as you stand on the brink of a new beginning, you deserve to know that there is hope.** There is light beyond the shadows, and your story is far from over.

This book is dedicated to you—the resilient survivor of domestic violence. It is a testament to your strength and an offering of guidance as you navigate the process of reclaiming your life. **Here, you will find not only practical**

1

advice but also emotional support and encouragement. It is written with the belief that you are worthy of love, healing, and a future filled with hope and joy.

The purpose of this book is simple yet profound: to walk alongside you as you rebuild your life. **Through each chapter, we will explore the intricate journey of healing and empowerment.** We will dive into recognizing the signs of abuse, reclaiming your worth, preparing for a safe exit, and so much more. **Every page is written with the understanding that your healing is a sacred and personal journey.**

In these pages, you will learn how to find strength in your vulnerability, how to rebuild your identity, and how to thrive beyond survival. We will discuss practical steps for safety and independence, we'll dive into the emotional aftermath of trauma and explore the transformative power of self-care and forgiveness. **You will discover that your story, while marked by suffering, is also one of profound resilience and incredible potential.**

As you turn these pages, I encourage you to take the first step toward a brighter future. The road ahead may seem daunting, but with each step you take, you move closer to the life you deserve. Embrace this journey with an open heart, knowing that you are not alone. There are countless others who have walked this path and emerged stronger, and their stories are a testament to the power of hope and healing.

Your journey is unique, and your strength is boundless. Believe in the possibility of a future filled with peace, joy, and fulfillment. **Know that you are worthy of all the love and happiness that life has to offer.**

Take this first step with courage, and let this book be a guide and a companion on your path to healing and empowerment. The road to reclaiming your life may be long and winding, but with each step forward, you will find yourself rising higher, finding strength you never knew you had, and stepping into a future brimming with possibilities.

May you find comfort in these words, strength in the knowledge that you are not alone, and hope in the promise of a brighter tomorrow. Together, we'll break the chains and embrace the future you were meant to have.

With love and unwavering hope,

Shannon Savoy

CEO Narc Free Living

Chapter 1:
Recognizing the Signs of
Domestic Violence

Domestic violence doesn't always start with a bruise, a broken bone, or something you can see. Often, it begins in the shadows—with words that wound your soul, with the quiet isolation that pulls you away from those who love you. It starts small—subtle put-downs, controlling behavior, and manipulations that seem like "love" at first. Slowly, almost imperceptibly, you find yourself trapped in a cycle that feels impossible to break. But remember, dear sister, **God never intended for you to live in fear or be diminished by anyone**. He created you for freedom, peace, and a life full of love.

The enemy works through lies, through darkness, and through fear. Domestic violence is a tool that the enemy uses to keep God's children bound, but Christ came to set the captives free (Luke 4:18). In order to break free, you first need to understand what's happening. It's important to recognize that this form of abuse is not your fault. **It is a** distortion of the love that God designed for marriage and relationships.

What is Domestic Violence?

Domestic violence is a destructive pattern of behavior used by one person to control and dominate another in a relationship. It's more than just physical violence; it includes emotional, psychological, financial, and sexual abuse. Abuse isn't just what happens to your body—it's what happens to your mind, your heart, and your spirit. The abuser uses fear, manipulation, and intimidation to exert control. This is not love.

God's love is patient and kind. Love does not dishonor others or seek to control them (1 Corinthians 13:4-5). Abuse violates everything God intends for relationships and should not be tolerated or excused.

Types of Domestic Violence

Domestic violence is a dark and multifaceted beast, manifesting in many forms that each inflict deep and lasting wounds. Understanding these forms is crucial because each one, while different in its methods, shares a common goal: to exert power and control over you. Let's dive into these forms with a passionate and empathetic heart, for each one tells a story of pain and suffering that must be confronted and healed.

Emotional Abuse: The Destruction of Self-Worth

Emotional abuse is a silent predator that prowls in the shadows of a relationship. **It starts with subtle, insidious whispers that chip away at your sense of self-worth.** Constant criticism, name-calling, belittling—these are not just hurtful words; they are a relentless assault on your soul. The abuser may accuse you of being the source of every problem, making you believe that you are at fault for the turmoil around you.

Psalm 139:14 tells us, "I praise you because I am fearfully and wonderfully made." But emotional abuse blinds you to this profound truth. It distorts your self-image, making you doubt your worth and your beauty. **You may find yourself trapped in a maze of self-doubt and despair, struggling to remember the vibrant person you once were.**

Emotional abuse can be the most deceptive form of violence, as it often leaves no visible marks but inflicts deep, unseen wounds on your heart and mind. **It is a war waged on your very identity, and it is crucial to recognize it for what it is: a violation of the inherent dignity that God has bestowed upon you.**

Physical Abuse: The Brutal Assault on Your Body

Physical abuse is the most overt and visible form of domestic violence. **It is the harsh reality of being hit, slapped, choked, burned, or subjected to other forms of physical harm.** Even if these acts of violence are infrequent, the looming threat of physical harm casts a dark shadow over your life.

Your body is described in Scripture as a temple of the Holy Spirit (1 Corinthians 6:19). No one has the right to desecrate this sacred space. The physical bruises may heal over time, but the emotional scars left by such violence can last a lifetime. The fear and pain of physical abuse strip you of your sense of safety and control, leaving you feeling vulnerable and exposed.

Financial Abuse: The Chains of Dependence

Financial abuse is a covert but devastating tactic used to control and manipulate. It can involve preventing you from working, controlling access to money, or creating a state of financial dependency that traps you in the relationship. The abuser uses money not as a means of support but as a weapon to wield power over you.

Philippians 4:19 reassures us that "my God will meet all your needs according to the riches of his glory in Christ Jesus." Yet, financial abuse seeks to undermine this promise, leaving you feeling helpless and trapped. By creating financial dependence, the abuser takes away your autonomy, making you reliant on them for necessities.

Psychological Abuse: The Assault on Your Reality

Psychological abuse is perhaps the most insidious form of domestic violence. It involves gaslighting, manipulating, and distorting your perception of reality to make you question your own judgment and sanity. The abuser sows seeds of doubt, causing confusion and emotional distress.

"For God is not a God of disorder but of peace" (1 Corinthians 14:33). Yet, psychological abuse turns your world upside down, shrouding it in confusion and turmoil. This form of abuse is a cruel mind game, designed to make you feel like you are losing touch with reality, making it even harder to break free.

Sexual Abuse: The Violation of Intimacy

Sexual abuse is a profound betrayal of the sacred bond intended for marriage. **It involves forcing you into unwanted sexual acts or using sex as a weapon to**

control and demean. This abuse distorts the beauty and sanctity of physical intimacy, turning it into a tool of pain and manipulation.

Your body is a sacred gift, created in the image of God. Sexual abuse violates this sacredness, using intimacy as a means of exerting control. **It is a profound betrayal of trust and a deep violation of your dignity.** In the face of such abuse, remember that God's design for intimacy is one of love, respect, and mutual joy—not manipulation and control.

A Path to Healing

Each form of domestic violence leaves its mark, but each can also be confronted with courage and faith. Understanding these types of abuse is a crucial step in recognizing their impact on your life. By shining a light on these dark corners, you can begin the process of healing and reclaiming your worth.

Remember, no matter how deep the scars or how tangled the chains, God's love is a source of hope and restoration. He does not leave you in the darkness but offers a path to healing and wholeness. As you embark on this journey, know that you are not alone and that the strength to overcome lies within you.

The Cycle of Abuse

In the shadowed corridors of domestic violence, one of the most insidious and painful aspects is the cycle of abuse—a relentless, cyclical pattern that traps its victims in a seemingly endless loop of fear and false hope. This cycle is not just a pattern of behavior; it is a profound, destructive force that seeks to erode your soul and break your will.

Understanding it is crucial to breaking free and reclaiming your life.

1. Tension Building: The Calm Before the Storm

The cycle often begins with a period of escalating tension. Small conflicts, seemingly insignificant at first, begin to grow. The abuser may start to exhibit signs of irritation, becoming increasingly critical or distant. You might find yourself walking on eggshells, desperately trying to diffuse the mounting tension and prevent an outburst.

Each day feels like a fragile balance between peace and chaos. You are caught in a web of anxiety, dreading the inevitable eruption. The atmosphere becomes charged with an unspoken fear, as if the air itself is heavy with the weight of impending doom.

The abuser's behavior may shift unpredictably, creating a sense of instability and confusion. It's a subtle manipulation, making you question yourself and your actions, as you try to appease someone whose anger seems to brew beneath the surface. You're not only trying to maintain peace but also grappling with a growing sense of helplessness.

2. Incident: The Explosive Outburst

The tension eventually explodes into an abusive incident. **The calm façade shatters violently, and what was once an atmosphere of tense anticipation becomes a storm of anger, pain, and fear.** This moment can manifest in various ways—verbal tirades that cut deep, physical violence that leaves bruises on your body and soul, or other forms of harm that devastate your sense of safety.

In these moments, you might feel as though your entire world has been upended. The incident leaves you feeling shattered, scared, and bewildered. **The once small, manageable cracks in your relationship have turned into gaping wounds.** It's as if a part of you has been torn away, leaving you exposed and vulnerable.

3. Reconciliation: The Deceptive Calm

Following the outburst, the abuser may attempt to reconcile. **They might apologize profusely, promise to change, or shower you with affection.** This phase can be particularly deceptive. The abuser's words and actions are designed to lull you into a false sense of security, to rekindle hope in a promise that history has shown to be hollow.

You may find yourself yearning to believe in the promises of change. The abuser's remorse feels like a balm to your wounded heart, and the temporary return to tenderness may seem like a glimmer of hope amidst the darkness. **But remember, these promises are often just another layer of manipulation designed to keep you trapped in the cycle.**

4. Calm: The Illusion of Peace

After the reconciliation, a period of calm follows—a deceptive tranquility that can feel like a breath of fresh air after a storm. **The calm might bring a fleeting sense of relief, but it's often just a temporary lull before the cycle begins anew.** The peace is fragile and superficial, masking the underlying volatility that still threatens to erupt.

This cycle of calm and chaos can make it incredibly difficult to break free. The temporary peace can create a false hope that things will improve, but without genuine change, the cycle is destined to repeat itself. You find yourself caught in a relentless loop of hope and despair, where each cycle tightens its grip on your spirit.

God's Love vs. The Cycle of Abuse

It's important to understand that God's love is fundamentally different from the abusive cycle you've experienced. In the cycle of abuse, control, fear, and manipulation reign supreme. But God's love, as revealed in Scripture, is a love that brings freedom, peace, and unconditional acceptance.

2 Corinthians 3:17 reminds us, "Now the Lord is the Spirit, and where the Spirit of the Lord is, there is freedom." God does not bind His children in cycles of fear and control. His love is a beacon of light, guiding you out of the darkness and into a life of true freedom and peace.

Recognizing the Red Flags

When you're immersed in an abusive relationship, recognizing the red flags can be incredibly challenging. **The signs of abuse can be subtle and insidious, making it difficult to see the full extent of the manipulation and control.** But as children of God, we are called to live in the light, not in darkness (Ephesians 5:8-9). **Shining a light on the truth is a crucial step toward breaking free.**

Here are some common red flags to watch for:

1. Isolation: The abuser may attempt to cut you off from friends, family, and social support. They might make you feel as though no one else cares for you, or that they are the only one you can trust. But remember, you are a part of the body of Christ, and you are never truly alone. God places people in our lives to support and uplift us, and you are worthy of that support.

2. Control: The abuser may monitor your movements, control your finances, or dictate how you spend your time. God created you with free will, and no one has the right to strip that away. You have the right to make choices about your own life and to live in a way that honors your dignity and autonomy.

3. Blame Shifting: The abuser may refuse to take responsibility for their actions, blaming you for their anger or violence. In Christ, you are not responsible for the sins of others (Romans 14:12). The blame and guilt placed upon you are not yours to bear. You deserve to be treated with respect and understanding, not as a scapegoat for someone else's behavior.

4. Fear: If you find yourself constantly afraid of triggering an outburst or walking on eggshells to avoid conflict, this is not the life God intends for you. **2 Timothy 1:7 assures us, "For God gave us a spirit not of fear but of power and love and self-control."** God's plan for your life is not one of fear and subjugation, but one of love, empowerment, and freedom.

Recognizing these signs is the first step toward breaking free from the cycle of abuse. Jesus said, "I have come that they may have life, and have it to the full" (John 10:10). Living in fear and control is not the fullness of life that He promised. You are precious in God's eyes, and you are worthy of love, safety, and peace.

As you begin to recognize and understand the cycle of abuse, know that you are not alone. With courage and faith, you can break free from this cycle and step into a life of healing and wholeness. God's love and grace are with you, guiding you toward a future filled with hope and restoration.

Chapter 2:
Understanding Your Worth and Power

When you've endured the relentless darkness of domestic violence, it can feel as though your very soul has been shattered. The cruel words, the suffocating control, the insidious manipulation—they don't just attack your body; they assault the very essence of who you are. Over time, this unrelenting storm chips away at your sense of self, leaving you battered and questioning *everything*. You may start to believe the monstrous lies whispered into your ear: "I'm not enough," "I deserve this," "No one will ever love me."

But these are not truths. They are the venomous lies of the enemy, crafted to ensnare you in a prison of despair and self-doubt. These lies seek to distance you from the boundless love and freedom that Jesus came to offer. In this chapter, we will embark on a profound journey to rediscover the intrinsic worth that is yours in Christ and reclaim the power that has always been yours, rooted in God's unwavering truth.

The Emotional Toll of Abuse and Its Impact on Self-Esteem

Abuse doesn't merely leave behind physical bruises—it etches deep, painful scars upon your emotional landscape. The abuser's cruel criticisms, relentless insults, and devious manipulations twist and warp your perception of yourself until you start to believe that you are less than what God created you to be. **The emotional toll of such abuse can make you feel broken, weak, and powerless. Yet, none of these feelings are true in the eyes of God.**

Psalm 139:14 declares, "I praise You because I am fearfully and wonderfully made; Your works are wonderful, I know that full well." This is the divine truth about you: You were crafted by God with profound love and intention, designed to reflect His image and His glory. Abuse seeks to rob you of this truth, to make you feel small and worthless, but God's Word stands as an unshakable foundation. **No person, no matter how they may treat you, can alter the value that God has already bestowed upon your life.**

The emotional damage of abuse manifests in various devastating ways:

Low Self-Esteem: The Erosion of Your Self-Worth

Imagine the emotional toll as a constant barrage of attacks on your self-worth. The abuser's relentless criticisms, the disparaging comments, and the belittling actions chip away at your confidence, leaving you with a shattered sense of self. Each insult, each harsh word is like a hammer blow to your self-esteem, making you question your value and your place in the world. You may start to

15

doubt your own worth, believing that you are unworthy of love or respect.

But remember, in God's eyes, you are immeasurably precious. **The harsh voices of the abuser are nothing but empty echoes compared to the resounding truth of God's love.** You are fearfully and wonderfully made, a masterpiece of divine creation.

Shame and Guilt: The Weight of Unwarranted Burdens

Shame and guilt are cruel companions in the aftermath of abuse. You may feel ashamed for staying in a situation that seems unbearable or guilty for wanting to leave, as if your desire for a better life is somehow wrong. These feelings are manipulative chains, designed to keep you tethered to the pain.

But God's love is not rooted in shame or guilt. He invites you to cast your burdens upon Him, to exchange your shame for His grace. There is no guilt in seeking freedom and healing; there is only the promise of redemption and renewal.

Fear and Anxiety: The Perpetual State of Terror

Fear becomes a constant, oppressive force in an abusive relationship. You live in a state of perpetual anxiety, never knowing what will set off the next outburst or what the future holds. The constant unpredictability creates a crippling fear that seeps into every corner of your life.

Yet, God's Word tells us, **"For God gave us a spirit not of fear but of power and love and self-control" (2 Timothy 1:7).** His plan for you is not one of terror but of strength, love, and peace. In Him, you have the power to overcome the paralyzing fear that seeks to dominate your life.

Hopelessness: The Despair of a Never-Ending Cycle

Hopelessness is perhaps the darkest shadow of all. You might feel trapped in a cycle that seems never-ending, believing that your current reality is the only one possible. The weight of this despair can be overwhelming, making you feel as if there is no light at the end of the tunnel.

But remember, Jesus came to give you life, and life in abundance (John 10:10). His promise is one of transformation and renewal. He offers you a future filled with hope, a future where you are not bound by the chains of your past but free to embrace the new life He has prepared for you.

Reclaiming Your Worth and Power

Amid such profound pain, it can be challenging to see beyond the immediate suffering. **But know this: your worth is not defined by the abuse you've endured.** It is defined by the love and grace of God, who sees you as His beloved child, worthy of all the good things He has in store for you.

As we journey through this book together, remember that you are not alone. With each step, we will uncover the truth of your worth and the power that has always resided within you. You are strong, you are valued, and you are deserving of a life filled with love, respect, and joy.

Take heart and embrace the truth that God has for you. Your past does not define your future, and the love of God is a beacon that will guide you towards healing and restoration. The journey to reclaiming your worth and power begins now, and it is a journey that leads to a place of profound freedom and fulfillment.

Chapter 3:
Reclaiming Your Identity and Voice

In the wake of domestic violence, the soul endures a profound and often invisible trauma. Each harsh word, each cruel act, tears at the very fabric of your being, attempting to erase your sense of self. Over time, the relentless assault on your identity may leave you feeling as though you are nothing but a shadow of the person you once were. The lies whispered in the dark corners of your mind— "I'm not enough," "I deserve this," "No one will ever love me"—are not just painful; they are designed to enslave you in a cage of despair and self-doubt.

But hear this, dear sister: God is close to the brokenhearted and saves those who are crushed in spirit (Psalm 34:18). No matter how deep the wounds of abuse, **God sees you, and He is ready to heal you.** This chapter is a beacon of hope, guiding you to reclaim the identity that has always been yours in Christ—a beautiful, unshakable identity that transcends the lies and the pain.

The Journey to Rediscover Your Identity

Abuse is a thief, a ruthless plunderer of the soul. It aims to steal your sense of self, leaving you to question your worth and purpose. You might find yourself tangled in a web of false beliefs, convinced that you are defined by the abuse you've endured. **But this is a lie.** You are not the sum of the insults hurled at you or the emotional scars inflicted upon your heart. **You are a beloved child of God, chosen and cherished before the foundation of the world (Ephesians 1:4).**

Your true identity is found in Christ, and nothing can alter the value that God has placed upon you. Abuse tries to blind you to this truth, making you feel small and insignificant. **Yet, God's Word stands firm, a steadfast anchor in the storm.** The love and grace of God are your reality, and they offer a path to healing and renewal.

Embracing the Truths of Scripture

To reclaim your identity, you must immerse yourself in the truth of God's Word. **Here are some powerful Scriptures to hold onto as you journey towards healing:**

- **You are loved: "See what great love the Father has lavished on us, that we should be called children of God! And that is what we are!" (1 John 3:1).**

"Yes, I have loved you with an everlasting love; Therefore with lovingkindness I have drawn you. (Jeremiah 31:3).

19

This love is not fleeting; it is a profound, eternal affection that defines who you are. No amount of abuse can diminish the depth of God's love for you.

- **You are valuable:** "Are not five sparrows sold for two pennies? Yet not one of them is forgotten by God. Indeed, the very hairs of your head are all numbered. Don't be afraid; you are worth more than many sparrows" (Luke 12:6-7). Your worth is immeasurable in God's eyes. You are precious, valued beyond comprehension.
- **You are strong in Christ:** "I can do all things through Christ who strengthens me" (Philippians 4:13). The strength you need to overcome the past and build a new future is available through Christ. He is your source of power and resilience.
- **You are chosen:** "You are a chosen people, a royal priesthood, a holy nation, God's special possession" (1 Peter 2:9). You are not an afterthought; you are chosen and set apart for a purpose that is both noble and sacred.

Reclaiming Your Voice

Abuse often tries to silence its victims, making you feel voiceless and powerless. **But your voice matters.** God has given you the power to speak truth, to set boundaries, and to stand against injustice. **In Christ, your voice is a tool for healing and transformation.** You have the authority to declare life and to challenge the lies that have sought to define you.

Here are practical exercises to help you reclaim your confidence and voice:

1. **Daily Affirmations in Christ:** Each morning, stand before the mirror and declare the truths of Scripture over yourself. Say aloud, "I am fearfully and wonderfully made. I am loved. I am chosen. I am strong in Christ." Let these affirmations replace the negative self-talk with the truth of who God says you are.

2. **Write a Letter to Your Future Self:** Pen a letter to yourself one year from now. Describe the strong, confident, and healed person you are becoming. **Visualize the peace you will feel and the ways God has worked in your life.** Seal the letter and set a date to open it in the future as a testament to your growth and transformation.

3. **Create a Gratitude Journal:** Start a journal where you record daily expressions of gratitude. **Focus on the small victories and blessings, no matter how minor they may seem.** Gratitude helps shift your perspective from what is broken to what is beautiful and abundant in your life.

4. **Surround Yourself with Godly Support:** Reach out to a support network that will uplift and encourage you. Whether it's a church group, a counselor, or trusted friends, or Narc Free Living, **seek out those who will speak life into you and remind you of your worth when you forget.** As Ecclesiastes 4:9-10 reminds us, "Two are better than one... if either of them falls down, one can help the other up."

5. **Practice Small Acts of Courage:** Rebuilding confidence is a gradual process. **Start with small**

steps outside your comfort zone. Set boundaries, voice your needs, and take small actions that affirm your growing strength. Each act of courage is a testament to your resilience and power.

6. **Prayer and Meditation on God's Word:** Dedicate time each day to prayer and meditation. Ask God to reveal His love for you and to help you see yourself through His eyes. **In the stillness of prayer, God will speak to your heart, reinforcing His deep love and care for you.** Psalm 46:10 says, "Be still, and know that I am God." In these moments of quiet reflection, let God's peace and assurance wash over you.

Embracing the Path Forward

Dear sister, even in the darkest depths of your suffering, God has never abandoned you. **He is the One who lifts your head, who restores your soul, and who heals the wounds that run so deep.** As you begin to reclaim your identity and rebuild your confidence, remember this profound truth: **God has already declared victory over your life.** The chains of fear and shame that once held you captive have been shattered in the name of Jesus, and you are free.

This is the beginning of your journey back to yourself, back to the radiant woman God created you to be. Trust in Him, lean on His promises, and embrace the future filled with hope and purpose that He has in store for you (Jeremiah 29:11). You are valuable, cherished, and powerful in His sight, and your journey towards healing and self-discovery is one of profound beauty and promise.

Chapter 4:
Preparing to Leave Safely

Leaving an abusive relationship is one of the most courageous and harrowing decisions you will ever make. It's a path fraught with uncertainty, fear, and emotional turbulence, but remember this immutable truth: **God has not given you a spirit of fear, but of power, love, and a sound mind (2 Timothy 1:7).** In the midst of this storm, you are not alone. God walks with you, and there are concrete steps you can take to ensure your safety and build a new life beyond the shadows of abuse.

Creating a Safety Plan

The foundation of leaving safely begins with a meticulously crafted safety plan. This is not merely a set of steps; it is a lifeline, a beacon of hope that guides you through the chaos and uncertainty of leaving an abusive situation. A safety plan empowers you with clarity and direction, giving you the strength to take that pivotal step toward freedom.

Identifying Safe Places and Trusted People

The first critical element of your safety plan is identifying safe places where you can go when the time comes. These are sanctuaries of peace, places where you can find refuge from your abuser's reach.

- **Safe Places:** Compile a list of locations where you can go immediately if you need to escape. These could be the homes of trusted friends or family members, or local shelters designed to provide immediate safety. **Keep this list hidden in a secure place, away from prying eyes.**

- **Trusted People:** Identify at least one or two individuals who understand your situation and can support you discreetly. These are people who can offer practical help without alerting your abuser to your plans. **Proverbs 11:14 reminds us, "Where there is no guidance, a people fall, but in an abundance of counselors, there is safety."** Pray for discernment in choosing these trusted allies, those who will walk beside you in this journey towards liberation.

Gathering Important Documents and Resources

Before you leave, it is crucial to gather all necessary documents and resources. These items are not just papers—they are keys to unlocking a new beginning, tools for establishing a life free from the constraints of abuse.

- **Identification:** Secure your driver's license, passport, and Social Security card. These documents are essential for starting anew and accessing various services.

- **Financial Documents:** Collect all financial records, including bank account information, credit cards, and any other pertinent financial documents.
- **Legal Documents:** Ensure you have copies of important legal documents such as birth certificates (for you and your children), marriage licenses, insurance papers, and any protective orders you have obtained.
- **Medications:** Gather enough medication for yourself and your children to last until you can access a new pharmacy.

Store these items in a secure, hidden location, or entrust them to a reliable friend or family member. **Having these documents ready is a crucial step in ensuring a smooth transition and securing your future.**

Financial Preparations: Saving Money and Accessing Resources

Financial control is a common tactic used by abusers to trap their victims in a cycle of dependency and fear. However, **God is Jehovah Jireh—the God who provides (Genesis 22:14).** Even in the bleakest circumstances, He will make a way for you to reclaim your independence and stability.

Saving Money

Start by setting aside whatever money you can, no matter how small the amount. Even modest savings can accumulate over time, providing you with a crucial financial cushion.

- **Set Up a Private Bank Account:** Open an account in your name only and choose paperless statements to keep it confidential. This account should be separate from any joint accounts with your abuser.

- **Save Small Amounts:** Store small amounts of cash in a secure location where your abuser cannot find it.
- **Find Financial Assistance:** Seek out organizations that offer financial support to survivors of domestic violence. Many shelters, charities, and churches provide funds for essentials like rent and food.

Accessing Resources

There are numerous resources available to support you as you leave. **God often works through communities and organizations dedicated to helping those in need.**

- **Local Shelters:** Many domestic violence shelters provide more than just a safe place to stay. They offer financial resources, counseling, and legal aid to help you rebuild your life.
- **Churches and Charities:** Reach out to local churches and charities, which may have benevolence funds or connections to additional resources.
- **Government Programs:** Explore government assistance programs for housing, food, and financial aid. These programs often prioritize survivors of domestic violence.

Technology Safety: Securing Devices, Social Media, and Online Accounts

In the digital age, technology can be both a lifeline and a potential danger. Abusers may use technology to track your movements or monitor your communications. **Securing**

your devices and online accounts is vital to maintaining your safety and privacy.

Securing Your Devices

To protect yourself from digital monitoring, take the following steps:

- **Change Your Passwords:** Update passwords for all your accounts—phone, email, social media, and financial institutions. Use strong, unique passwords for each account.
- **Turn Off Location Tracking:** Disable location services on your phone and social media platforms. Ensure that GPS features are turned off to prevent your abuser from tracking your whereabouts.
- **Use a Safe Device:** If you suspect your phone or computer is compromised, use a different device for important communications or resource searches. Consider using a public library computer or a phone from a trusted friend.

Social Media Safety

Social media can be a double-edged sword, providing both connection and potential danger:

- **Change Your Privacy Settings:** Make your social media profiles private, and limit who can view your posts and personal information.
- **Be Cautious About Posting Your Location:** Avoid sharing real-time locations or tagging yourself in posts to prevent your abuser from tracking your movements.
- **Consider a Temporary Break:** If necessary, temporarily deactivate your social media accounts

to protect yourself from being monitored or harassed.

Resources Available: Shelters, Hotlines, and Legal Support

There is no shame in seeking help. In fact, it is a testament to your strength and wisdom. God often sends aid through others, and there are many organizations dedicated to supporting survivors of domestic violence.

Shelters

Domestic violence shelters offer immediate protection and a range of support services. Many provide counseling, legal assistance, and resources to help you start anew. Contact a local domestic violence hotline or search online for shelters in your area.

Hotlines

National and local hotlines offer 24/7 support. These hotlines can provide advice, information about resources, and emotional support as you navigate this challenging time.

Embracing the Path Forward

Leaving an abusive relationship is a monumental act of courage, and each step you take towards safety is a victory in itself. Remember, God is with you in every moment of this journey, guiding and protecting you. As you prepare to leave, trust in His provision and seek out the resources and support you need to rebuild your life.

You are not alone. The path may be fraught with challenges, but with faith and preparation, you will find your way to a future filled with hope and freedom. God has already paved the way for your liberation, and His promises will sustain you through every trial.

Here are some trusted hotlines:

- **National Domestic Violence Hotline**: 1-800-799-SAFE (7233)
- **National Coalition Against Domestic Violence:** 1-844-237-2331
- **Local hotlines:** Many cities and states have local hotlines that provide resources and direct assistance.

Legal Support

When the darkness of abuse surrounds you, seeking legal protection becomes a crucial beacon of hope. In the labyrinth of legalities and paperwork, the path to freedom can seem daunting, but remember this: God is a God of justice, who deeply desires to see you safe and liberated (Isaiah 61:8). His divine justice is not only a promise but a guiding light in your darkest hour.

If you find yourself in need of legal protection, such as a restraining order, know that there are organizations ready to stand with you. These organizations offer free legal services specifically designed for survivors of domestic violence, helping you navigate the complexities of the legal system with compassion and expertise. Reaching out to a local domestic violence agency, shelter, or legal aid organization can connect you with the resources you need to secure your safety and reclaim your life.

Imagine this: You are standing at the edge of a precipice, where the pain of your past and the uncertainty of the future converge. But in this moment, God extends His hand, offering you the support and protection of those who are dedicated to ensuring your freedom and safety. They are equipped to fight for your rights, to help you obtain the legal orders necessary to keep you safe from harm, and to provide the legal counsel you need to forge a new path.

As you prepare to leave, let this truth resonate deeply within your heart: God is your refuge and strength, an ever-present help in times of trouble (Psalm 46:1). He is not a distant observer but an active protector, intricately involved in every aspect of your journey towards liberation. His presence is a sanctuary in the storm, a steady hand guiding you through the turbulence of your circumstances.

You are not walking this path alone. Surrounding you are people—both seen and unseen—who are ready to support you, to offer their resources, and to fight alongside you in the pursuit of justice. Each step you take towards freedom is a testament to your strength, resilience, and faith. Though the journey may be fraught with challenges, every step is a stride towards a future where safety and dignity are restored.

Embrace the support available to you, lean on the resources that stand ready to assist you, and trust in the One who holds your future in His hands. In every moment of doubt and fear, remember that God's love for you is boundless and unchanging. He is with you, fiercely protecting you and guiding you towards the promise of a new beginning.

Your safety, your freedom, and your peace are worth every effort. Let this journey be marked not by the shadows of your past, but by the light of hope and the assurance of a brighter, safer future. Trust in God's provision and the power of His justice, and know that you are deeply loved and protected as you step into this new chapter of your life.

Chapter 5:
The Exit Strategy: Leaving the Abuser

The moment has arrived—a moment steeped in both dread and exhilaration. Leaving an abuser is not just a decision; it's a courageous act of reclaiming your life from the clutches of fear and control. This is a monumental step, a declaration of your right to safety and peace, but it requires careful, strategic planning. Your heart may be screaming to run, but now is the time for calm, calculated action.

How to leave safely?

This is where meticulous planning becomes your greatest ally. Every detail matters. Your escape must be deliberate, precise, and as invisible as possible. You can't afford to be reckless, even though every fiber of your being may be urging you to flee. Here's how to craft a plan that prioritizes your safety and minimizes risks:

1. Choose a Safe Time

The moment of your departure should be a silent, well-orchestrated escape. Timing is crucial. Aim to leave when your abuser is least likely to notice your absence—when they're at work, asleep, or otherwise out of the house. Silence becomes your greatest ally. Any hint or confrontation before you leave can escalate danger and jeopardize your safety. Resist the impulse to give any forewarning or engage in a confrontation. This is about making a clean break, ensuring that your departure is swift and undetected.

Visualize the departure: Picture every step from the moment you leave the house to when you arrive at your safe location. This mental rehearsal will prepare you for the critical moments ahead.

2. Have an Escape Route

Your escape route is the lifeline that will lead you to safety. Know precisely where you'll go—whether it's a trusted friend's home, a local shelter, or a safe house provided by an organization. Map out your route meticulously. Imagine it in your mind, from start to finish. Ensure you can navigate this route quickly and safely, without unnecessary delays or risks.

If possible, practice the route during times when your abuser isn't around. Familiarity with the path will reduce anxiety and increase your confidence during the actual departure.

3. Pack an Emergency Bag

Preparation is key to a smooth escape. Pack an emergency bag with essentials that will sustain you and your children in the immediate aftermath of your departure. This bag should include:

- Identification documents: Driver's license, passport, Social Security card.
- Financial resources: Cash, bank cards, and any financial documents.
- Medications: Enough medication for yourself and your children to last until you can access new prescriptions.
- Clothing: A change of clothes for you and your children, along with any other personal items that are vital.

Store this bag in a place where your abuser cannot access it but is still easy for you to reach when the moment comes. This might be with a trusted friend, hidden in a secure spot, or in a location that is easy for you to access quickly.

4. Cover Your Tracks

Secrecy is crucial in your exit strategy. Leaving no trace of your plans will protect you from the abuser discovering your intentions. Here's how to cover your tracks:

- Delete messages: Remove any digital traces of your plans. Delete texts, emails, and any communications that might alert your abuser.
- Turn off location tracking: Disable GPS and location services on your phone and social media accounts to prevent your abuser from tracking your movements.

- Avoid sharing plans: Refrain from discussing your escape with anyone who might inadvertently reveal your plans to the abuser.

Leaving is not just a physical act; it's a profound spiritual journey. Just as God parted the Red Sea for the Israelites, making a way where there seemed to be no way, He will pave a path for you through the darkness. His protection surrounds you, and His guidance will lead you safely through the perilous transition.

The Role of Law Enforcement and Restraining Orders

In the gravity of your exit strategy, law enforcement may become an essential component of your safety. While the idea of involving the police can be intimidating, their support might be crucial in ensuring your immediate safety.

1. Call for Help

If you find yourself in immediate danger, do not hesitate to call 911. Your safety and the safety of your children come first. The police are equipped to help remove you from the dangerous situation, escort you to safety, and assist in gathering any essential belongings. They are trained to handle such emergencies and can provide crucial protection in these critical moments.

2. Restraining Orders

For many survivors, obtaining a restraining order is a vital step in maintaining safety after leaving. A restraining order, also known as a protection order, legally forbids the abuser from contacting or approaching you. If the abuser violates this order, law enforcement has the authority to intervene and enforce the law. Ensure you keep copies of the restraining order with you at all times for your protection.

Remember, as you seek legal protection, the battle is not merely legal—it is deeply spiritual. As you file those papers, appear in court, and stand firm in your truth, know that God is with you. "The Lord will fight for you; you need only to be still" (Exodus 14:14). He stands beside you, fighting on your behalf, making a way through the wilderness of your struggle.

You are stepping into a new chapter—one where courage, faith, and the divine assurance of God's protection converge. Every step you take towards freedom is a testament to your strength and resilience. As you move forward, trust in the divine plan that unfolds before you, knowing that God's love and protection are with you every step of the way. Your journey to safety and freedom is not just an escape; it is a declaration of your right to live in peace, to embrace a future filled with hope, and to claim the life that you so deeply deserve.

How to Seek Immediate Shelter and Help

The thought of walking out the door can be terrifying. **Where will you go? Who will help you?** The enemy will whisper doubts, trying to keep you in the grip of fear, but God's promise rings louder: **"The name of the Lord is a fortified tower; the righteous run to it and are safe"** (Proverbs 18:10). When you take that step, you are not walking alone.

There are **shelters and safe houses** specifically for survivors of domestic violence. These places are designed to provide immediate refuge, often at undisclosed locations to ensure your safety. They will offer you a bed, meals, and often legal assistance, counseling, and other critical resources to help you start rebuilding.

How to find shelter:

- **National Domestic Violence Hotline**: Call 1-800-799-SAFE (7233) for immediate help in locating a shelter near you. The hotline is confidential and available 24/7.
- **Local organizations**: Many cities and towns have local domestic violence organizations that offer shelter, counseling, and legal aid. They can help guide you through the process and provide the immediate support you need.
- **Churches**: Some churches have networks or ministries designed to assist women and children fleeing abuse. Don't hesitate to reach out to a trusted faith community for help.

Tips for Protecting Children During This Process

As much as your heart aches for yourself, it aches even more for your children. **How can you protect them in the midst of this storm?** Their safety and emotional well-being are paramount, and there are steps you can take to ensure they are protected as you make your escape.

1. **Keep the plan a secret**: Depending on your children's age and ability to understand, it's essential to shield them from the details of the plan until the moment comes. If they're too young to understand, make the escape process feel as normal as possible—packing a bag with their favorite toys,

telling them they're going to a friend's or family member's house for a visit.

2. **Reassure them with God's promises**: Children may feel afraid, confused, or anxious about leaving. **Speak to them in words of faith and hope.** Remind them that God is watching over them. "The Lord is my light and my salvation—whom shall I fear?" (Psalm 27:1). Keep a Bible with you, and read to them during moments of fear.

3. **Involve them in the safety plan**: If they are old enough, explain the safety plan in a way they can understand. Teach them to dial 911 in an emergency and give them a code word that signals they need to leave or hide. Make sure they know where to go if things escalate.

4. **Keep their routine**: Children thrive on routine, and while leaving an abuser disrupts life, **try to maintain some sense of normalcy**—their favorite blanket, bedtime prayers, or morning rituals can provide a sense of security in the midst of chaos.

5. **Seek counseling for them**: Children exposed to domestic violence may carry the trauma with them. As soon as you're able, seek counseling or support groups specifically designed for children who've witnessed abuse. God desires to heal not only your wounds but theirs as well.

This is the storm before the calm—the darkness before the dawn. But in these moments, know that you are covered by the mighty hand of God. **You are leaving the chains of abuse behind, stepping into a new life where fear no longer rules, and safety becomes your new reality.** The road ahead may be difficult, but as you walk out of the shadows and into the light, you are walking toward a future of hope, freedom, and peace.

Remember the words of Jesus: "**In this world you will have trouble. But take heart! I have overcome the world**" (John 16:33). He has overcome your circumstances, and He will see you through. You are strong, you are brave, and you are not alone.

Chapter 6:
Restraining Orders vs. Protective Orders

While the terms "restraining order" and "protection order" are often used interchangeably, they can have key differences depending on the jurisdiction. Both are legal instruments designed to help protect individuals from threats, harassment, or abuse, However, the two types of orders differ substantially in both how they are applied by courts and enforced by police departments.

In most cases, protective orders are connected to incidents of family violence and are issued when someone has experienced assault, harassment, or abuse, including stalking and sexual violence. Meanwhile, restraining orders are generally tied to civil legal matters and aren't usually related to criminal cases.

What is a Protective Order?

A protective order is issued by the court when there is a clear and immediate threat of violence. This violence can take various forms, including domestic abuse, sexual assault, or threats of violence. The primary purpose of these orders is to safeguard victims from ongoing abuse or contact that may escalate to violence.

In cases of family violence, a protective order typically mandates the following actions against the alleged abuser:

- Cessation of physical abuse.
- Prohibition against making threats of any kind.
- A ban on contacting you, your children, or other household members.
- A requirement to maintain a specific distance from you, your children, your home, your workplace, and your children's school.
- Cessation of interference with the care, custody or control of a pet or companion animal.
- A restriction on carrying firearms, which may include suspending any licenses to carry weapons.
- Additionally, law enforcement has the authority to arrest anyone who violates the terms of a protective order.

How Does a Protective Order Safeguard Me and My Children?

In the movie *Enough*, Jennifer Lopez's character asks a police officer about the effectiveness of a protective order, humorously questioning if it's just "a little piece of paper" that stops someone from coming near. This sentiment captures the hesitation many feel when considering a protective order in abusive situations.

Protective orders are specifically intended to minimize the chances of future threats or harm from someone who poses a risk. Protection orders frequently include additional provisions for child custody, financial support, and other issues related to domestic life, whereas restraining orders may focus solely on restricting contact and proximity.

While they aren't foolproof and can't guarantee complete safety, they do carry serious consequences for violations. These can include jail time, substantial fines, and even prison sentences for the alleged abuser if they breach the order. Ultimately, protective orders serve as a vital tool in enhancing your safety and that of your children.

How Long Will My Protective Order Last?

There are three types of protective orders related to family violence, though the specifics may vary by state or jurisdiction. Here's a breakdown of the types:

Temporary Ex Parte Protective Order

If you've experienced abuse or assault in the past and believe it could happen again, you can seek a temporary ex parte protective order with the assistance of a domestic violence attorney.

To obtain this order, you must demonstrate that:

- You have been abused by your partner.
- There is a reasonable fear that you may face further abuse.

Once the evidence is reviewed, a judge can issue the protective order for a limited duration, typically up to 21 days. The term "ex parte" indicates that the order can be granted without a hearing, providing immediate protection while the other party is served and both parties await a formal hearing.

Final or Permanent Protective Order

During the hearing, the court may issue a protective order that can last for up to five years (again this depends on your state or jurisdiction. In instances of severe or chronic abuse, the court may even grant lifetime protective orders.

Magistrate's Order of Emergency Protection (commonly known as an emergency protective order)

The first two types of protective orders mentioned are issued by a civil court based on your application, and the abuser does not need to be arrested for these to be granted. In contrast, the third type is typically issued by a criminal court following the abuser's arrest. Emergency protective orders can be effective for a duration ranging from 30 to 91 days, depending on the specific situation.

An emergency protective order may be issued if your partner has committed offenses such as:

- Assault
- Stalking
- Sexual abuse
- Sexual assault
- Trafficking

This order can be requested by you, your guardian (if applicable), the police officer who made the arrest, or the prosecutor. Usually, it is filed by the arresting officer at the time of arrest.

What is a Restraining Order

It is a legal directive from the court that prohibits a person from engaging in specific behaviors, clearly detailing what actions are allowed and which are not. These orders are formally documented and filed alongside other court records to ensure compliance during legal proceedings. It's important to note that restraining orders are associated with civil cases rather than criminal ones. Restraining orders are generally broader in scope and may also cover disputes beyond domestic violence, including business conflicts, neighbor disputes, and more.

How Are These Orders Enforced?

Restraining orders cannot be enforced through criminal law, meaning law enforcement cannot take action based solely on a violation. Instead, the individual affected must return to court to seek a civil remedy. During this court appearance, a hearing will take place, and the judge will make a ruling based on the evidence provided. If the order is violated, the judge may impose financial penalties or additional restrictions to further limit the offender's access or contact with the petitioner.

In contrast, violations of protective orders can lead to criminal consequences, such as jail time or fines, and in some cases, they may be classified as felonies, resulting in more severe penalties. However, violating a restraining order typically does not lead to criminal charges, but it may result in monetary sanctions imposed by the court.

Both orders can be powerful tools in safeguarding survivors of abuse but knowing which one to file depends on your specific situation. It's crucial to seek legal counsel to ensure you pursue the appropriate form of protection for your safety and well-being.

Chapter 7:
After the Escape: Rebuilding
Your Life

The door slams shut behind you, and in that echo, you find the first taste of freedom. For the first time in what feels like an eternity, the chains of your captivity are gone. The world outside is no longer a cage but a vast expanse of possibilities, and yet, the freedom you fought so hard to achieve comes with a whirlwind of emotions—joy intertwined with fear, relief mingled with uncertainty. The dark night has ended, and you've emerged into the light of day, but the journey is far from over.

This is the part they don't prepare you for, the aftermath of escape—a tumultuous sea of triumph and grief, relief and terror. The battle doesn't end with your departure; in many ways, it has just begun. This new chapter of your life is a land of both hope and challenge, where every step forward is a testament to your resilience and courage.

Managing the Emotional Aftermath: Guilt, Fear, and Freedom

As the dust settles and the silence envelops you, guilt begins to creep in like a shadowy intruder. You find yourself trapped in an endless loop of self-doubt and remorse. Questions haunt you in the quiet moments: Did I make the right choice? Could I have stayed longer? Was there something more I could have done to fix the situation? You replay every fight, every tear, every moment of helplessness with the haunting belief that perhaps, somehow, you should have been able to change things.

But listen closely to this truth: You did not deserve the abuse. You were never responsible for the cruel and destructive actions of another. Leaving was not an act of failure but the bravest decision you could have made—for yourself and for your children. The enemy of your soul will try to ensnare you in the trap of guilt, but remember, guilt is not a tool of God. He has set you free, and there is no condemnation for those who are in Christ Jesus (Romans 8:1). Embrace this freedom from the chains of blame and shame. You have taken the monumental step of liberation, and you are worthy of peace and healing.

Yet, alongside guilt, fear clings to you like a second skin. Even though the physical threats are gone, the emotional shadows remain. You wonder: What if they find me? What if they come after me? Every sound becomes a potential danger, every knock on the door a reason to jump. The fear feels like a relentless companion, always lurking just out of sight. But let the Word of God speak louder than the trembling fears within you: "God has not given us a spirit of fear, but of power and of love and of a sound mind" (2 Timothy 1:7).

Your journey towards freedom is not a sprint but a marathon of healing and rebuilding. The fear may not vanish instantly, but with each passing day, as you lean into God's promises and embrace His strength, the fear will lose its grip on your heart. Freedom is both a blessing and a challenge. You are no longer bound by someone else's control, yet this newfound liberty brings with it a host of choices and uncertainties.

Where will you go from here? What will you do with this precious gift of freedom? Who are you now that you've broken free from the past? These questions are not meant to overwhelm you but to guide you gently toward your new life. Only time and grace can provide the answers, but take solace in knowing that God is guiding you through this uncharted territory.

The Path Forward: Embracing the Journey

In the quiet moments after your escape, the world feels both vast and intimidating. The freedom you sought is now yours, but it comes with the responsibility to rebuild your life, to rediscover who you are without the shadow of abuse. Embrace this process as a journey of rediscovery and renewal.

Allow yourself to grieve the loss of the life you thought you would have and acknowledge the pain that comes with such a profound change. Yet, amidst this grief, let hope take root. Each day is an opportunity to create something new, to build a life filled with possibility and joy.

Seek support from those who understand your journey—therapists, support groups, and trusted friends. Surround yourself with a community that uplifts and encourages you, providing the strength you need to navigate this new chapter.

Celebrate the small victories, the moments of clarity and joy. Each step forward is a testament to your courage and resilience. And remember, you are not alone in this journey. God walks with you, guiding your steps, comforting your heart, and providing the strength you need to face each day.

You are walking into a future where you have the power to shape your destiny, to build a life of peace and fulfillment. Embrace this journey with the confidence that you are worthy of love, joy, and safety. Your freedom is not just a new beginning; it is the chance to rewrite your story with grace, strength, and the unwavering assurance that God is with you every step of the way.

The Importance of Therapy, Counseling, Coaching, and Support Groups

In the quiet aftermath of your escape, you might feel the overwhelming need to process your emotions, to find a way to heal the deep wounds that abuse has inflicted. It's crucial to remember that you don't have to face this alone. Healing from trauma is not a solitary journey but one best traveled with the support and guidance of those who understand your pain.

Therapy is a vital part of this healing process. A licensed therapist, particularly one experienced in trauma and domestic violence, becomes a beacon in the tumultuous sea of emotions you're navigating. Imagine sitting across from someone who listens with compassion and understanding, who helps you untangle the emotional knots—fear, anger, sadness, and guilt—that have been tightly bound by years of abuse. This is where you will find the safe space to finally exhale, to voice the pain and fear that you have long been silenced against. Your story, full of raw and untold truths, deserves to be heard. Therapy offers you that sacred sanctuary.

Counseling extends this healing process further by aiding in the reconstruction of your identity. Abuse strips away your sense of self, leaving you with a fractured view of who you are—small, powerless, and worthless. But remember, God knows who you truly are. He fashioned you with purpose and beauty, declaring you fearfully and wonderfully made (Psalm 139:14). Counseling helps you rediscover the woman God created you to be—strong, resilient, and profoundly loved. Through counseling, you begin to rebuild your sense of self-worth, piece by piece, reclaiming the person you were always meant to be.

Coaching plays a vital role in the recovery process after narcissistic abuse. At Narc Free Living LLC, I offer coaching from a biblical perspective. A Bible-based coach helps survivors transform from victims into empowered victors through the Word of God, guiding them toward both spiritual and emotional freedom. Coaching provides structure, strategy, prayer, and direction during a time when survivors often feel lost, overwhelmed, or unsure of how to move forward. After abuse, survivors may struggle with trust, identity, or self-worth, and a coach can help navigate these complex emotions.

A coach offers validation, strategies, and a non-judgmental, empathetic space to help survivors reclaim their power by affirming their experiences and reinforcing their self-worth. We work with you to develop personalized action plans that support recovery and promote growth. Coaches also hold survivors accountable for their progress while providing consistent support and encouragement.

Support groups provide a unique and invaluable element to this journey: community. Here, you will find others who have walked the same path, who have faced similar battles and emerged victorious. The power of shared experience cannot be overstated. In these gatherings, you'll meet women who understand your pain without judgment, who offer solidarity and encouragement. It's a sisterhood forged in the fires of survival, a group that will cheer you on as you piece together the fragments of your life, one courageous step at a time.

I founded Chain Breaker University (CBU) mentorship, Rock Your Crown, Domestic Violence In The Church, Safety After Abuse, Healing Father & Mother Wounds, Healing From Heartbreak & Beyond, Dating After Narcissistic Abuse, and various other survivor events and workshops, all designed as safe spaces & support groups where narcissistic abuse survivors can heal and thrive together.

Building a New Home and Creating a Safe Space

After years of living under the oppressive shadow of abuse, the thought of creating a new home can seem daunting. But this is your opportunity to forge something new, to establish a sanctuary where peace, safety, and love can flourish.

Your new home doesn't need to be perfect or grand. It could be a modest apartment, a room in a shelter, or a corner of a friend's house. What matters is that it is yours—free from the fear and control that once dominated your life. As you fill this space with things that bring you comfort—soft blankets, family photos, your favorite books—you're not merely decorating; you are reclaiming your life. Each item you place is a symbol of your newfound freedom and autonomy.

Create peace in your new space. Let your home be infused with serenity and hope. Pray over your living space, inviting God's presence to fill it with His peace and protection. Adorn your walls with Bible verses that remind you of His promises of safety and provision. Let the soothing melodies of worship music play, creating an atmosphere of healing and grace. This space is now your sanctuary—a haven where you can breathe deeply, rest fully, and embrace your freedom.

Navigating the Legal System: Custody, Divorce, and Financial Independence

As if the emotional and spiritual battles weren't enough, you now face the daunting task of navigating the legal system. The process of divorce, custody battles, and achieving financial independence can feel like climbing a steep, unyielding mountain. Yet, these steps are crucial in fully severing ties with your abuser and establishing your new life.

1. **Custody:** If you have children, your fight extends beyond your own safety to ensure their protection and well-being. The courtroom can become a battlefield where their future is at stake. Seek legal counsel, and, if possible, find an advocate who specializes in domestic violence cases. God is your

ultimate defender, and He will fight for you and your children, ensuring their safety and your peace of mind.

2. **Divorce:** For many survivors, divorce is the final act of severing the bonds that once tied you to your abuser. It can be a painful process, particularly if your abuser attempts to manipulate or retaliate through legal channels. Yet, remember this: while the legal system may be a battleground, the spiritual victory is already yours. God is a God of justice, and He will guide you through this process, providing strength and clarity as you navigate the legalities.

3. **Financial Independence:** Abuse often leaves you financially constrained, but now is the time to reclaim your financial freedom. Start small, taking steps to rebuild your financial stability. Open a bank account in your name, explore assistance programs if needed, and seek employment or training opportunities. Whether it's securing a job, enrolling in a training program, or applying for grants, trust that God is your provider. He will supply all your needs according to His riches in glory (Philippians 4:19).

As you step into this new chapter of your life, remember that the journey is one of transformation and growth. Each challenge you face, each obstacle you overcome, is a testament to your strength and resilience. God walks with you every step of the way, guiding you, providing for you, and affirming your worth. Embrace this new beginning with faith and courage, knowing that the path ahead is filled with the promise of healing, hope, and a future brimming with possibilities.

Rebuilding your life after escaping abuse is not just a journey—it is a spiritual transformation through the uncharted territories of your mind, heart, and soul. It is a path littered with the rubble of your past, yet illuminated by the glimmering possibilities of a future filled with hope and renewal. As you embark on this profound journey, understand that it requires not only patience and faith but also a wellspring of resilience that flows from the depths of your spirit, sustained by God's grace. Through Him, healing and recovery become possible.

There will be days when the weight of your past feels like an anchor dragging you down, when the scars of your experiences seem too heavy to bear. On those days, the echoes of the abuse may haunt you, whispering shadows of doubt and fear. Yet, in these moments of overwhelm, when the darkness of your past looms large, remember that you are not walking this treacherous path alone.

God walks beside you, a steadfast companion through the storm. He is the guiding light that pierces through the fog of despair, the protective shield that guards you from the remnants of your past tormentors. His presence envelops you, His hand upholds you, and His love saturates every step you take. This new chapter of your life is not simply about survival—it is about flourishing, about embracing a destiny that transcends the pain and sorrow you once knew.

This journey is about becoming the woman God intended you to be—a woman free from the chains of abuse, living in the radiant light of His love and grace. It is about rediscovering your strength, redefining your identity, and reclaiming your sense of purpose. As you navigate this transformative period, each day brings you closer to the fullness of life that awaits you, a life where your worth is no longer defined by the cruelty of others but by the boundless love of your Creator.

And one day, when you look back on this journey, you will see a mosaic of courage, strength, and redemption. You will witness the resilience it took to leave behind a life of darkness, the fortitude required to rebuild from the ashes of your past, and the sheer beauty of a life lived in the freedom you have fought so hard to attain. You will recognize the hand of God in every triumph, every tear, and every victory, understanding that He was with you all along, guiding you through the wilderness to a place of peace and fulfillment.

This is your story—a story of redemption, of freedom, of a relentless spirit that refused to be broken. It is a testament to the power of faith and the unwavering belief that even in the darkest of times, there is light. Embrace this journey with confidence and hope, knowing that each step forward is a step closer to a life of profound joy and unshakable peace. Your story is not just one of survival; it is one of magnificent transformation.

Chapter 8:
Breaking the Trauma Bond

You've left. The physical chains have been shattered, the oppressive grip of the abuser is no longer a daily torment, but you find yourself inexplicably tethered to them, emotionally ensnared despite the miles that now separate you. It's a haunting paradox that baffles those around you. They see the evidence of your suffering—the bruises, the scars, the emotional wreckage—and they struggle to understand why letting go is still so painfully elusive.

But only you can feel the weight of the invisible chains that bind you. This bond, deeply rooted in the anguish and fleeting affection of your past, is known as a trauma bond. Breaking it may well be one of the hardest and most profound battles of your life. Yet, it is a battle that can and will be won. Remember, God's grace is boundless, and His strength is made perfect in your weakness.

Understanding Why It's So Hard to Leave Emotionally

Leaving an abusive relationship is not just a physical departure; it is an intricate and tumultuous emotional, psychological, and spiritual journey. Abuse crafts a unique and sinister attachment—a trauma bond—that lingers long after the bruises have healed and the threats have ceased.

At the heart of this bond lies a cruel cycle of pain and intermittent reward. The abuse is punctuated by sporadic moments of tenderness—an unexpected gesture of kindness, a heartfelt apology, a promise of change. These fleeting glimpses of hope become addictive. They create a shimmering illusion of potential change, convincing you to believe that perhaps, against all odds, things could improve. Each new promise ignites the cycle again, strengthening the emotional tie that binds you.

This emotional rollercoaster wreaks havoc on your mental and emotional well-being. Your psyche becomes accustomed to the highs that follow the lows, much like an addiction. The abuser, paradoxically, becomes both your source of agony and the sole provider of relief. In this toxic symbiosis, your sense of reality becomes distorted. You begin to question your worth, your strength, and your ability to survive independently.

But here is the unvarnished truth: this bond is not love. It is control, fear, and manipulation masked as affection. True love does not deconstruct your spirit; it nurtures and elevates it. It does not corrode your self-worth but builds you up in the light of truth and strength. Recognizing this bond as a construct of control rather than affection is crucial to dismantling it. Your scars are not definitions of who you are—they are mere testaments to what you've survived.

Healing from the Attachment to the Abuser

Breaking the trauma bond demands a profound and courageous process of healing. It starts with facing the stark reality of your relationship—the truth that has been obscured by years of deceit and manipulation. This is a painful journey, requiring you to confront the lies that kept you imprisoned, the manipulation that clouded your judgment, and the fear that still grips your soul. As the Bible so powerfully states, "the truth will set you free" (John 8:32).

1. **Name the Pain:** Voice your truth, even if it begins with whispering it to yourself. Acknowledge the reality of your suffering: "I was abused. I was manipulated. I was hurt." Naming your pain breaks the silence and begins to unravel the false narratives that have imprisoned your self-worth.

2. **Sever the Covenant and Soul Ties:** You may leave the relationship physically, but the spiritual covenant and soul ties remain intact until they are severed spiritually and naturally. Pray a prayer to sever all ungodly covenants and soul ties. Make a renewed covenant with God to be your provider, Father, friend, and advocate through the Blood of Jesus. Renounce all ungodly soul ties and ask God to heal your wounds. (1 Samuel 18:1)

3. **Forgive Yourself:** Survivors of abuse often carry a burdensome guilt. You might feel ashamed for staying as long as you did or blame yourself for not escaping sooner. But remember this: the abuse was

never your fault. Forgive yourself for the time it took to escape, and for the love you gave to someone undeserving. God forgives you, and He calls you to extend that forgiveness to yourself.

4. **Trust God's Healing:** You are not alone in this healing process. God is your ultimate healer, comforter, and guide. Psalm 34:18 promises, "The Lord is close to the brokenhearted and saves those who are crushed in spirit." Trust that God is working in your heart, even when the pain seems insurmountable. Healing is a journey, not an instantaneous cure, but God's love remains steadfast, guiding you through every step.

Techniques for Emotional Detachment and Self-Care

Breaking a trauma bond is both a spiritual and practical endeavor. Here are steps to begin emotionally detaching from your abuser and reclaiming your sense of self:

1. **No Contact or Minimal Contact (if possible):** The primary step in severing the trauma bond is to minimize or eliminate contact with your abuser. If you can, go no contact—block phone numbers, cut off social media, and avoid any form of communication that might pull you back into the cycle. If children or legal matters require some form of interaction, keep it strictly professional and limited to necessary communications, using text or email when possible and setting firm boundaries.

2. **Surround Yourself with Support:** Isolation was a tool of your abuser, but now is the time to reconnect with your community. Lean on friends, family, or

support groups who understand and support your journey. Let them remind you of your inherent worth and strength, and the vibrant life you are building apart from your abuser.

3. **Journaling:** Writing can be a powerful way to detach emotionally. When you feel the pull of the trauma bond, write about it. Chronicle your pain, grieve the lost relationship, and document the new life you are creating. This process helps clarify your emotions and gives you a sense of control over your narrative.

4. **Daily Affirmations:** Speak life and truth over yourself daily. Replace the lies you've been fed with God's promises. Declare affirmations such as:
   - "I am fearfully and wonderfully made" (Psalm 139:14).
   - "I am loved by God, and nothing can separate me from His love" (Romans 8:38-39).
   - "I am strong, courageous, and able to face whatever comes my way" (Joshua 1:9). Let these truths become the soundtrack of your healing journey.

5. **Engage in Self-Care:** Trauma takes a toll on both mind and body. Self-care is essential, not selfish. Find what nourishes your soul, whether it's prayer, worship, nature walks, or creative pursuits. Allow yourself the grace to rest, heal, and rediscover joy.

Stories from Survivors Who Overcame Trauma Bonds

You are not alone in this struggle. Many women have walked your path, wrestled with similar emotional chains, and emerged stronger, freer, and more whole. Their stories stand as beacons of hope and proof that the trauma bond can be broken, and true healing is possible.

Selena's Story: "I stayed because I believed he could change. Every apology, every fleeting moment of kindness made me cling to hope. But I knew deep down something was wrong. Therapy helped me realize I was ensnared in a trauma bond. I had to confront the excuses I made and face the painful truth. It was the hardest step, but breaking free was the beginning of my true healing. I now understand that love doesn't hurt—it uplifts."

Kim's Story: "The emotional connection was so intense; I felt I needed him to survive despite my misery. After leaving, I found strength in my faith and joined a support group. Meeting other survivors showed me that what I had was not love but control. I broke free, and I'm forging a new path, never looking back."

Breaking the trauma bond is not a single act; it is a continuous process. It demands time, courage, and unwavering faith. With each day, you grow stronger, moving further away from the person who tried to break you. As you traverse this path, remember that God's love is your anchor. He will never leave you nor forsake you (Deuteronomy 31:6). In Him, you will find the strength to break free, the grace to heal, and the love that truly liberates. You are no longer bound to your past. You are a cherished child of God, stepping into the fullness of His promises and walking in the light of His eternal love.

Chapter 9:
Rebuilding Trust and Healthy Relationships

The wounds of abuse do not merely fade away with your departure from the tormentor. They run deep, leaving indelible scars etched onto your heart, mind, and soul. One of the most excruciating parts of your healing journey is learning to trust again—not just others, but yourself. After the betrayal of someone who was supposed to love you, it is only natural to feel hesitant, guarded, and even fearful of opening your heart to anyone again. But remember this: God did not create you to live in fear or isolation. He fashioned you for connection, for love, and for relationships rooted in His grace and respect.

Rebuilding trust may seem like an insurmountable challenge, but with patience and faith, you can forge relationships that reflect the true love, respect, and grace that God intended for you.

How to Trust Again After Abuse

Emerging from the shadow of abuse, the idea of trusting anyone—even yourself—can feel daunting and almost unattainable. Your trust was shattered by someone who exploited your love and vulnerability. The betrayal you experienced may make you question if anyone is truly trustworthy or if you will ever feel safe in a relationship again. But amidst this despair, there is hope. God is the great restorer, capable of mending what was once broken.

6. **Trust Yourself Again:** One of the initial steps in rebuilding trust is reconnecting with and trusting yourself. Abuse can distort your judgment, leaving you doubting your instincts and decisions. You may question your ability to discern danger or to safeguard yourself. Yet, you are not powerless. Recognize that you have already made one of the most courageous decisions of your life: you left the abuser. You chose freedom and reclaimed your strength. Psalm 73:26 assures us, "My flesh and my heart may fail, but God is the strength of my heart and my portion forever." Trust that God is guiding you, and as you lean on Him, He will grant you wisdom to navigate future relationships. Embrace the freedom to make mistakes and learn from them, without succumbing to guilt or shame. You are evolving, healing, and rediscovering how to trust yourself once more.

7. **Take Small Steps with Others:** Rebuilding trust with others is a gradual process. It is not about plunging into deep relationships immediately but rather taking small, deliberate steps. Begin with individuals who have consistently shown

themselves to be trustworthy—whether they are family members, friends, or mentors. Let them into your life incrementally. Allow trust to develop naturally over time, without forcing it. Proverbs 3:5-6 advises us to "Trust in the Lord with all your heart and lean not on your own understanding; in all your ways submit to Him, and He will make your paths straight." As you open yourself to new people, let God guide your heart and direct your steps.

8. **Pray for Discernment:** Trust does not equate to blind faith in everyone you meet. Abuse may have taught you to be hypervigilant or overly suspicious, but healthy trust involves wise discernment. Pray earnestly for discernment in your relationships. Ask God to reveal the true intentions of those you encounter and to guide you in setting appropriate boundaries. Invite the Holy Spirit to lead you as you navigate new friendships and potential relationships, ensuring that your trust is anchored in wisdom and divine guidance.

What a Healthy Relationship Looks Like

Recognizing what constitutes a healthy relationship can be challenging after experiencing abuse. Abuse distorts your perception of love, making it difficult to differentiate between healthy and unhealthy dynamics. But true love is neither complex nor manipulative; it is simple, nurturing, and rooted in respect.

1. **Mutual Respect:** In a healthy relationship, respect is paramount. Both partners honor each other's boundaries, feelings, and autonomy. There is no place for control or dominance. Respect involves

listening to one another's perspectives, even in disagreement, and valuing each other's opinions without belittling or manipulating. It means appreciating each other's individuality and treating one another with dignity.

2. **Trust and Honesty:** Trust is the bedrock of any healthy relationship. Both partners are honest and transparent, without deceit or hidden agendas. Trust means being open with each other and having faith in one another's commitment and integrity. It means creating a space where vulnerability is met with understanding and where honesty is the norm.

3. **Support and Encouragement:** A healthy relationship thrives on mutual support. Each partner encourages the other's growth, dreams, and well-being. There is no room for jealousy or sabotage—only genuine care for each other's happiness and success. Both individuals uplift and motivate one another, celebrating achievements and offering comfort during challenges.

4. **Equality:** Equality is fundamental in a healthy relationship. There is no power imbalance or unilateral decision-making. Both partners share responsibilities and decisions, respecting each other's autonomy. No one person dictates the terms of the relationship or imposes their will on the other. Both individuals are empowered to be their authentic selves.

5. **Healthy Conflict Resolution:** Disagreements are a natural part of any relationship, but in a healthy relationship, conflict is resolved with respect and effective communication. There is no place for name-calling, yelling, or threats. Both partners can express

their feelings and concerns without fear of retaliation or abuse. Conflict resolution is approached with empathy, understanding, and a commitment to finding solutions together.

1 Corinthians 13:4-7 beautifully encapsulates the essence of healthy love: "Love is patient, love is kind. It does not envy, it does not boast, it is not proud. It does not dishonor others, it is not self-seeking, it is not easily angered, it keeps no record of wrongs. Love does not delight in evil but rejoices with the truth. It always protects, always trusts, always hopes, always perseveres." Let this passage serve as the benchmark for any relationship you pursue moving forward.

Rebuilding trust and forging healthy relationships is not a swift or simple process. It demands time, patience, and steadfast faith. Each day you grow stronger, inching closer to relationships that reflect the true essence of love and respect. As you embark on this journey, remember that God's love is your steadfast anchor. He will guide you through the turbulence, provide the grace to heal, and offer the strength to build relationships that embody His divine love. You are not condemned to live in isolation or fear. You are a beloved child of God, destined to experience the fullness of His promises and the richness of relationships defined by His love.

Setting Boundaries and Recognizing New Red Flags

Emerging from the darkness of abuse, you may feel like you're stepping into the sunlight for the first time. But as you begin to navigate this new world, one crucial task lies before you: setting healthy boundaries. These boundaries are not walls meant to isolate you; rather, they are protective barriers designed to preserve your emotional, physical, and spiritual well-being. They are a declaration of your needs and expectations, an assertion of your autonomy in relationships, and a safeguard against falling back into harmful patterns.

Defining Your Boundaries

In the aftermath of abuse, understanding and defining your boundaries is essential. Your inner child needs healing, and setting boundaries is a part of that process to keep you safe. Take a moment to reflect deeply on what you need to feel safe and valued in your relationships. Ask yourself: Is this person emotionally safe for me? What behaviors are unacceptable to me? How much emotional availability can I offer right now? What level of intimacy am I comfortable with? What are my deal-breakers?

It's not about perfection; it's about clarity and self-awareness. This process of defining boundaries is a form of self-care and empowerment. It allows you to enter new relationships with a clear sense of what you will and will not tolerate. It's a declaration of self-worth, a promise to honor your own needs and protect your heart from further harm.

Communicating Boundaries Clearly

Once you have a firm grasp on your boundaries, the next step is to communicate them effectively. Approach this task with firmness and respect. Be clear about your needs and expectations, and do so with a sense of confidence. Your boundaries are not negotiable; they are a vital part of your self-preservation and recovery.

If someone crosses these boundaries, address the issue immediately. It's crucial to uphold your limits with courage and integrity. If a person refuses to respect your boundaries, consider it a significant red flag. Their unwillingness to honor your needs is indicative of a potential threat to your well-being. Remember, boundaries are not about punishing others but about safeguarding your own heart and soul.

Watching for New Red Flags

Leaving an abusive relationship doesn't mean that unhealthy dynamics will vanish. It's imperative to remain vigilant for new red flags that might signal potential abuse or manipulation. Some common warning signs to be aware of include:

- **Overly Controlling Behavior:** Beware of anyone who tries to dictate your time, decisions, or friendships. This behavior reflects a desire for control rather than genuine respect.
- **Jealousy and Possessiveness:** Pay attention to individuals who constantly accuse you of cheating or attempt to isolate you from your support network. These actions are attempts to undermine your independence and autonomy.
- **Love-Bombing:** Be cautious of someone who overwhelms you with excessive affection and attention early in the relationship. This intense and unsustainable dynamic can mask deeper issues and lead to manipulation.
- **Lack of Respect for Boundaries:** Watch for individuals who ignore or challenge your boundaries, attempting to guilt or manipulate you

into compromising them. True respect means honoring the limits you set.

- **Quick Attachment:** Be wary of someone who rushes the relationship or becomes overly invested too soon. Healthy relationships take time to develop trust and intimacy naturally.

Trust your instincts. If something feels off or makes you uncomfortable, it's crucial to step back and reassess. Protect yourself from further harm by listening to your intuition and seeking clarity.

Building a Support System of Friends, Family, and Community

Healing from abuse is not a solitary journey. It is essential to surround yourself with a support system of people who genuinely care about your well-being. God designed us for community, and having a strong network of support can profoundly impact your journey to healing and wholeness.

1. **Lean on Friends and Family:** If you have friends or family members who have been supportive throughout your experience, now is the time to reach out to them. Allow them to offer emotional support, and let them help you rebuild your sense of trust and connection. They can remind you of your worth and provide the safety and care that your abuser could never offer.

2. **Join Support Groups:** Consider joining a support group for survivors of abuse. Hearing from others who have walked a similar path can be incredibly healing. These groups offer a safe space to share your story, gain insights, and realize that you are not

alone. The shared experiences and collective wisdom of others can provide comfort and guidance.

3. **Find Community in Faith:** Church communities can be a powerful source of support for survivors. Seek out a church that values love, grace, and emotional healing. Surround yourself with people who will pray with you, encourage you, and walk alongside you on your path to restoration. God created you for connection, and He will guide you to relationships that bring life and support. Ask God to lead you to the right church and community.

4. **Build New Friendships:** As you heal, you may find that some of your previous relationships no longer serve you. That's okay. Allow space for new friendships to develop—ones that are rooted in mutual respect, love, and trust. Open your heart to new people who value you and support your growth.

Rebuilding trust and forming healthy relationships is a gradual process that requires patience, discernment, and faith. Each step you take towards setting boundaries, recognizing red flags, and nurturing supportive connections brings you closer to the life God intended for you. You are worthy of love, respect, and joy. With every boundary you set, every moment of discernment you practice, and every new connection you foster, you are constructing a future founded on the truth of who you are—a cherished child of God, deserving of healthy, life-giving relationships. Trust that God will continue to guide and protect you as you rebuild your life. In Him, all things are made new, and every day is an opportunity to embrace the fullness of His promises.

Chapter 10:
Empowering Yourself for the
Future

After breaking free from the shadow of an abusive relationship, you may find yourself standing on the precipice of a new beginning. The future, once shrouded in fear and uncertainty, now beckons with a mix of daunting challenges and exhilarating possibilities. You've endured the unspeakable, but now, you are poised to reclaim your life, rediscover your purpose, and embrace a future brimming with hope and promise.

As you step into this new chapter, remember this: you are not defined by the suffering you endured. You are defined by the extraordinary courage it took to leave, the resilience that continues to fuel your journey, and the unwavering strength that will guide you forward. God's plans for you are filled with hope and a future (Jeremiah 29:11). It is time to empower yourself to seize all that lies ahead, to build a life that reflects the dignity and worth you have always possessed.

Career and Financial Independence

One of the most profound ways to reclaim your life after abuse is through financial independence. Abusers often exert control over finances to keep their victims trapped, stifling their ability to make their own choices and live free from manipulation. Breaking free from that financial control is a monumental step towards gaining autonomy over your economic future. It is about more than just making ends meet; it is about liberating yourself from the chains that bound you and stepping into a life of true freedom.

1. Identify Your Skills and Strengths

Take a deep breath and reflect on your skills, talents, and passions. Even if your abuser tried to diminish your confidence or convince you of your inadequacy, you possess unique gifts that are waiting to be unleashed. Whether you have experience in a specific trade, administrative skills, or a flair for creativity, there are countless opportunities for you to explore.

Pray for divine guidance as you contemplate your strengths. Ask God to reveal the path He has prepared for you. Proverbs 16:9 reminds us, "The heart of man plans his way, but the Lord establishes his steps." Trust that as you take proactive steps towards your goals, God will illuminate paths you never imagined. Embrace the journey with faith, knowing that each step brings you closer to a future filled with purpose and fulfillment.

2. Seek Employment, Start a Business, and Develop a New Skill Set

Depending on your situation, the journey towards financial independence may begin with finding immediate employment or pursuing further training to enhance your skills. Don't be discouraged by starting small—every step you take towards financial self-sufficiency is a step towards freedom and empowerment. Reach out to local organizations, career centers, or job placement services that can assist you in finding opportunities or provide training programs tailored to your needs.

Remember, it's never too late to learn and grow. If pursuing further education or job training is necessary for your career aspirations, explore the myriad resources available to you. Online courses, community colleges, and vocational training programs offer pathways to new skills and opportunities. Look into scholarships, grants, or financial aid options to make education more accessible. Embrace the opportunity to expand your horizons and build a career that aligns with your passions and goals.

3. Build Financial Literacy

Financial empowerment goes beyond securing a job—it involves mastering the art of managing your finances wisely. Begin by creating a detailed budget that outlines your income, expenses, and savings goals. Educate yourself on the principles of budgeting, saving, and investing. Financial literacy programs, budgeting apps, and financial advisors can offer invaluable guidance as you navigate this new territory.

If you had shared finances with your abuser, you may need to focus on rebuilding your credit or regaining control of your bank accounts. Don't hesitate to seek professional advice to help you understand and manage your financial situation. Remember, regaining control over your finances is not just about numbers—it's about reclaiming your power and securing a future where you are the master of your destiny.

Embracing Your Power and Purpose

As you embark on this journey of empowerment, remember that you are a force to be reckoned with. The abuse you endured does not define your worth or limit your potential. You are a survivor, a warrior, and a testament to the unbreakable spirit that resides within you. God's plans for your life are filled with hope, purpose, and boundless possibilities.

Embrace this new chapter with open arms and a heart full of faith. Each step you take towards independence, each skill you develop, and each financial milestone you achieve brings you closer to the life you deserve. Trust in the divine guidance that has led you to this point and know that God will continue to illuminate your path.

In this journey of empowerment, you are not alone. The strength you've found within yourself, the support of your faith, and the hope of a brighter future will guide you through every challenge and triumph. Embrace the opportunities that await, for they are a testament to your resilience and the promise of a future filled with purpose and joy.

Your journey is a powerful reminder that even in the darkest moments, there is always the possibility of a new beginning. You are a living testament to the transformative power of courage and faith. Step forward with confidence, knowing that your future is bright, your dreams are valid, and your life is a canvas awaiting the masterpiece of your new beginnings.

Pursuing Education and Skill-Building

Education and skill-building are not just tools; they are keys to unlocking the future you've always desired. They represent a journey from a past marked by control and limitation to a future brimming with possibility and self-determination. Each step you take towards learning and growth is a step towards a life where you are in charge of your destiny.

1. Continuing Your Education

Returning to education can feel like an insurmountable challenge, especially if it has been years since you last sat in a classroom. Yet, this act of courage can be transformative. Whether you're seeking a college degree, completing high school, or acquiring new technical skills, education is a powerful pathway to new opportunities. It's a chance to rediscover and rekindle the passions and dreams that may have been suppressed by the weight of abuse.

Don't let fear or self-doubt hold you back. There are numerous programs designed specifically for adult learners, many of which offer the flexibility to accommodate your needs. Look into scholarships and support groups dedicated to survivors of abuse—they can provide not just financial assistance, but also the encouragement needed to embark on this new journey.

2. Building Marketable Skills

Formal education is not the only route to empowerment. Many career paths value practical skills and hands-on experience just as much as, if not more than, academic credentials. Online learning platforms like Coursera, Udemy, or LinkedIn Learning offer a wealth of affordable courses in areas such as technology, marketing, and design. These platforms provide the flexibility to learn at your own pace, allowing you to develop new skills from the comfort of your home.

Consider vocational programs or apprenticeships that offer practical training in fields like healthcare, construction, culinary arts, or beauty services. These programs provide invaluable experience and can lead directly to job opportunities. The key is to remain committed to learning, growing, and developing skills that enhance both your career prospects and personal life.

Developing Long-Term Goals and Dreams

After enduring years of control and manipulation, your long-term goals and dreams may have felt like distant memories. Yet, God's purpose for you remains steadfast, and He longs to restore the vision you once had for your life. Now is the time to rediscover your passions, set new goals, and pursue the future you deserve.

1. Dream Big

You have endured the unimaginable, and now it's time to reclaim your dreams. What aspirations have you kept hidden away? What goals did you once hold dear before the abuse took hold? Allow yourself to dream once more. Whether it's starting your own business, writing a book, traveling the world, or creating art, your dreams are valid and vital.

Write down your goals—both grand and modest—and start plotting a course to achieve them. Remember, nothing is too great for God. Ephesians 3:20 assures us that God is able to do "immeasurably more than all we ask or imagine." As you pursue your dreams, trust that God will guide you, providing the strength and support needed to turn your aspirations into reality.

2. Set Achievable Milestones

The path to achieving long-term goals requires patience and persistence. Break down your larger dreams into smaller, manageable milestones. This could involve completing a course, saving a specific amount of money, or networking with professionals in your desired field. Each milestone achieved brings you closer to your ultimate vision.

Celebrate your progress, no matter how small. Each victory, whether it's a completed project or a new skill learned, deserves recognition. You have earned the right to acknowledge and rejoice in your accomplishments.

Empowering Others and Becoming an Advocate

As you continue to heal and grow, you have a unique opportunity to use your experience to empower others. Your journey through pain and recovery has equipped you with a profound strength and perspective that can inspire and support those still trapped in the darkness of abuse. Becoming an advocate or mentor is a powerful way to transform your pain into purpose.

1. Share Your Story

One of the most impactful ways to help others is by sharing your story of survival and empowerment. Your journey can offer hope and encouragement to those who feel trapped in their own cycles of abuse. Whether you share your story within a support group, through social media, or on a public platform, your voice has the power to make a difference.

Remember, even in our darkest moments, God uses our experiences to bring light and hope to others. 2 Corinthians 1:4 tells us that God "comforts us in all our troubles, so that we can comfort those in any trouble with the comfort we ourselves receive from God."

2. Become an Advocate

If you feel called by God to do so, consider becoming an advocate for domestic violence survivors. This might involve volunteering at local shelters, working with advocacy organizations, or lobbying for policy changes that protect and support survivors. Your voice is powerful, and by speaking out against abuse, you can help others find their own strength and courage.

3. Mentoring Other Survivors

As someone who has walked the path of healing, you possess wisdom and insights that can guide others through their own journeys. Consider offering mentorship to survivors who are just beginning to rebuild their lives. Provide them with the support, encouragement, and love that you might have needed during the early stages of your recovery.

Your story is more than a tale of survival; it is a testament to triumph. You have faced and overcome the darkest moments of abuse, and now you stand empowered, ready to embrace a future filled with hope, strength, and purpose. Embrace your newfound power, pursue your dreams with unwavering faith, and continue to inspire others with your resilience and courage. Your journey into a brighter, more beautiful life is just beginning.

As you move forward, hold fast to the truth that you are worthy, powerful, and profoundly loved. With God's guidance and your own steadfast resolve, you will build the life you've always dreamed of, rising to inspire and empower others along the way. This is not just the end of a chapter—it is the dawn of a new era in your life, marked by faith, resilience, and boundless possibilities.

Chapter 11:
Living Free: Thriving Beyond Survival

Emerging from the suffocating grasp of abuse is a monumental triumph, a testament to your strength, resilience, and unyielding spirit. But now, as you stand on the precipice of a new beginning, it's time to embrace a life that's not just about surviving but truly thriving. The journey ahead is not just about navigating past pain but about embracing a future where joy, peace, and fulfillment reign supreme. This chapter is a celebration of your newfound freedom—a call to live a life where you're no longer defined by the shadows of your past but by the radiant promise of the future.

Finding Joy and Peace in Everyday Life

Having weathered the storm, you now have the opportunity to experience the serenity and joy that life has to offer. Finding joy and peace in everyday life involves recognizing and savoring the small victories, cherishing moments of happiness, and learning to appreciate the present with all its beauty.

1. Embrace Small Moments

Joy is often found in the seemingly mundane, in the quiet moments that can easily be overlooked. Take time to fully experience these moments, whether it's the warmth of a cup of coffee in the morning, the gentle rustle of leaves on a walk through the park, or the simple pleasure of a heartfelt conversation with a friend. These everyday experiences, though small, can hold profound meaning and bring deep peace and happiness.

Philippians 4:4 encourages us, "Rejoice in the Lord always. I will say it again: Rejoice." Let this verse be a reminder to find joy in the daily blessings of life. Even in the smallest of moments, there is a reason to rejoice, to celebrate the beauty of the present and the hope of the future.

2. Create Joyful Moments

Incorporate moments into your routine to bring a sense of stability and joy into your life. These rituals can be as simple as a weekly movie night with loved ones, a daily practice of journaling your gratitude, or a monthly adventure to discover new places. Such rituals create a space where you can reconnect with yourself and nurture your happiness.

3. Pursue Your Passions

Reignite your connection with activities and hobbies that once brought you joy or discover new interests that set your soul alight. Pursuing your passions can infuse your life with a sense of purpose and fulfillment. Whether it's painting, writing, dancing, or gardening, engaging in activities that make your heart sing is a powerful way to affirm your worth and embrace the fullness of life.

Healing from Past Trauma Through Self-Care

Healing from trauma is a profound journey that requires dedicated self-care. Self-care transcends mere physical wellness; it's a holistic approach that nurtures your emotional, mental, and spiritual well-being. It's an act of love and respect for yourself, acknowledging that you are deserving of care, attention, and compassion.

1. Prioritize Your Well-being

Make self-care an essential part of your daily life. This means more than just attending to physical needs; it encompasses regular exercise, balanced nutrition, ample rest, and engaging in activities that bring you joy. Self-care is about setting boundaries, ensuring you have time to recharge and renew yourself, and creating a life that honors your well-being.

2. Seek Professional Help

Healing often requires support from professionals who can provide guidance and tools to navigate your emotional landscape. Therapists and counselors are equipped to help you process past experiences, manage your emotional responses, and build healthier patterns of thought and behavior. Don't hesitate to seek out this support; it's a vital step in your journey towards healing.

3. Practice Self-Compassion

Be gentle with yourself as you move through the healing process. Understand that healing is not a linear journey; there will be setbacks and challenges along the way. Offer yourself the same compassion and understanding that you would extend to a dear friend. Psalm 147:3 assures us, "He heals the brokenhearted and binds up their wounds." Trust in this divine promise and recognize that you are deserving of this healing.

Practicing Gratitude and Mindfulness

Gratitude and mindfulness are transformative practices that help shift your focus from past pain to present joy. They ground you in the moment and foster a deep appreciation for the life you are living now.

1. Keep a Gratitude Journal

Start a gratitude journal to record the things you're thankful for each day. This practice encourages you to shift your perspective towards the positive aspects of your life, helping you appreciate the blessings that surround you. Psalm 136:1 says, "Give thanks to the Lord, for he is good. His love endures forever." Reflecting on your blessings deepens your connection to the goodness in your life and opens your heart to joy.

2. Embrace God's Presence

Remember the privilege of God's presence. Enjoy being fully present and aware of God's presence in each moment. Scripture encourages us to "be still, and know that I am God" (Psalm 46:10). You can practice by focusing and meditating on God's Word, or engaging in daily activities with gratitude and prayer. This practice becomes second nature, helps you connect with the present, appreciate God's blessings as they unfold, and foster a deeper sense of peace and contentment through His grace.

3. Engage in Acts of Kindness

Extending kindness to others can amplify your own sense of well-being. Engage in acts of kindness, whether they are grand gestures or small, everyday actions. Helping others creates a sense of fulfillment and connection, enhancing your overall happiness and reinforcing the positive impact you can have on the world around you.

As you step into this new phase of your life, remember that you are not merely rebuilding—you are thriving. You have navigated the darkness, and now you stand in the light, ready to embrace a future filled with joy, peace, and purpose. Living free means finding beauty and fulfillment beyond the shadows of your past. It's about celebrating the life you've fought so hard to create, pursuing your passions, and sharing your newfound strength with others.

Hold onto the truth that you are worthy of a life filled with love, joy, and endless possibilities. With each step you take towards embracing your future, you are not just surviving—you are living fully, thriving, and inspiring others with your resilience and courage. Your journey is a testament to the power of faith, hope, and the unbreakable spirit within you. This is your time to shine, to live free, and to flourish beyond the confines of survival.

Inspiring Others with Your Story

Your journey from the shadows of survival to the light of thriving is not just a personal triumph; it is a beacon of hope for countless others who are still lost in darkness. Your experiences, marked by courage and resilience, hold the power to inspire and uplift those who are struggling to find their way. By sharing your story, you transform your pain into a source of strength for others, illuminating a path from suffering to healing and renewal.

Share Your Journey

The act of sharing your story is an empowering step in both your own healing and the healing of others. Consider the myriad ways you can reach out and make an impact. Whether through writing a book, giving speeches, or utilizing the expansive reach of social media, your voice holds the power to reach hearts and minds. Each word you share can offer solace to someone who feels alone, each revelation can provide clarity to those navigating similar struggles.

Your story is not just a recounting of events; it is a narrative of hope and transformation. It's a testament to the strength of the human spirit and the power of overcoming adversity. By opening up about your journey, you invite others to see beyond their immediate pain, offering them a glimpse of the possibility that lies ahead. You have the extraordinary ability to turn your experiences into a lifeline for others, helping them find their way from the darkness to the dawn.

Mentor and Support

With the wisdom gained from your journey, you are uniquely positioned to mentor those who are embarking on their own path to recovery. Offering guidance, empathy, and practical support can profoundly impact someone who is just beginning their journey of healing. Your compassion can serve as a lantern in the night, guiding others through their darkest hours.

Mentorship is not just about providing advice; it's about offering a hand to hold and a heart that understands. Your experiences can lend credibility and reassurance to those who are feeling lost. By sharing your insights and strategies for coping and rebuilding, you empower others to forge their own paths to recovery. Your presence can be a source of comfort and a reminder that healing, though challenging, is not only possible but achievable.

Advocate for Change

Becoming an advocate for domestic violence survivors allows you to extend your influence beyond individual mentoring to effecting broader societal change. Your voice can contribute to crucial awareness campaigns, support legislative efforts, and collaborate with organizations dedicated to improving the lives of survivors. Advocacy is a powerful tool for addressing systemic issues and fostering environments where survivors are supported and protected.

Your commitment to advocacy signifies a dedication to creating a world where future generations are spared the suffering you endured. By working with established organizations, participating in community outreach, and pushing for policy changes, you become a catalyst for transformation. Your actions contribute to a larger movement towards justice and healing, ensuring that survivors' voices are heard and their needs are addressed.

Romans 8:28 reminds us, "And we know that in all things God works for the good of those who love him, who have been called according to his purpose." In sharing your story and advocating for others, you are embodying this divine promise. Your efforts are a manifestation of God's purpose for your life, channeling your experiences into a force for good that uplifts and empowers.

Living free is not about erasing the past but about embracing a future rich with joy, peace, and purpose. As you continue to heal and evolve, let your life serve as a testament to the incredible strength and resilience that lies within you. Your journey, marked by triumph over adversity, is a beacon of hope and a source of inspiration.

Embrace each day with a heart full of gratitude and mindfulness. Celebrate your victories, no matter how small, and pursue your dreams with unwavering faith and determination. Your life is a powerful narrative of overcoming, and through it, you possess the ability to inspire others, offering them hope and light in their darkest moments.

Live boldly, live freely, and let your light shine with God's glory. Your story is a testament to the extraordinary strength and beauty within you. As you continue to move forward, may you find joy in every moment, purpose in every step, and the fulfillment of seeing your journey transform into a source of hope and inspiration for others. Your life is a radiant example of the power of healing and the boundless potential for new beginnings.

Prayer Points for Escaping Narcissism

1.   **Deliverance from Manipulation:** Pray for God's deliverance from the manipulative tactics of the narcissist, seeking freedom from their control.

"For He has rescued us from the dominion of darkness and brought us into the kingdom of the Son He loves." – Colossians 1:13

2.   **Wisdom in Decision-Making:** Ask for wisdom, clarity, and a strategy to make the right decisions about leaving the abusive situation.

"If any of you lacks wisdom, you should ask God, who gives generously to all without finding fault, and it will be given to you." – James 1:5

3.   **Protection and Safety:** Pray for God's protection and safety as you navigate the process of escaping, ensuring you are shielded from harm.

"The Lord will keep you from all harm—He will watch over your life." – Psalm 121:7

4.   **Strength to Stand Firm:** Seek strength and courage to stand firm against the narcissist's attempts to lure you back or intimidate you.

"Be strong and courageous. Do not be afraid; do not be discouraged, for the Lord your God will be with you wherever you go." – Joshua 1:9

5.   **Supportive Connections:** Ask God to bring supportive friends, family, and resources into your life to aid in your escape and recovery.

"Two are better than one, because they have a good return for their labor: If either of them falls down, one can help the other up." – Ecclesiastes 4:9-10

6.   **Clear Mind:** Pray for a clear and focused mind to see the situation for what it truly is and to act with purpose and resolve.

"Do not conform to the pattern of this world, but be transformed by the renewing of your mind. Then you will be able to test and approve what God's will is—His good, pleasing and perfect will." – Romans 12:2

7.   **Healing of Emotional Wounds:** Request healing for the emotional wounds inflicted by the narcissist, allowing you to move forward with peace.

"He heals the brokenhearted and binds up their wounds." – Psalm 147:3

8.   **Provision of Resources:** Ask for provision of financial, legal, and logistical resources necessary for a successful escape.

"And my God will meet all your needs according to the riches of His glory in Christ Jesus." – Philippians 4:19

9.   **Breaking of Soul Ties:** Pray for the breaking of unhealthy soul ties and emotional bonds with the narcissist.

"The prayer of a righteous person is powerful and effective." – James 5:16

10.   **Freedom from Fear:** Seek freedom from fear and anxiety about the unknowns that come with leaving the abusive relationship.

"For God has not given us a spirit of fear, but of power, love, and a sound mind." – 2 Timothy 1:7

11.   **Divine Intervention:** Ask for divine intervention in your situation, trusting God to handle any obstacles that arise.

"The Lord will fight for you; you need only to be still." – Exodus 14:14

12.   **Renewed Identity:** Pray for a renewed sense of identity and self-worth, grounded in God's truth and love.

"Therefore, if anyone is in Christ, the new creation has come: The old has gone, the new is here!" – 2 Corinthians 5:17

13.   **Guidance in Planning:** Seek guidance and clarity in planning your exit strategy to ensure it is safe and effective.

"In their hearts humans plan their course, but the Lord establishes their steps." – Proverbs 16:9

14.   **Courage to Speak Up:** Ask for the courage to speak out about your situation and seek help from trusted individuals.

"The righteous are as bold as a lion." – Proverbs 28:1

15.   **Discernment of Intentions:** Pray for discernment to recognize and avoid any deceptive attempts by the narcissist to manipulate or sabotage your plans.

"But the one who is spiritual discerns all things, yet he himself is discerned by no one." – 1 Corinthians 2:15

16.   **Emotional Resilience:** Request emotional resilience to withstand the challenges and stress that come with leaving an abusive relationship.

"Cast all your anxiety on Him because He cares for you." – 1 Peter 5:7

17.   **Protection from Retaliation:** Ask for protection from any potential retaliation or harm from the narcissist after your departure.

"No weapon forged against you will prevail, and you will refute every tongue that accuses you." – Isaiah 54:17

18.   **Safe Environment:** Pray for a safe and supportive environment to transition into after leaving the abusive relationship.

"You are my hiding place; You will protect me from trouble and surround me with songs of deliverance." – Psalm 32:7

19.   **Healing of Relationships:** Seek healing for any damaged relationships caused by narcissistic abuse, both with yourself and others.

"Be kind and compassionate to one another, forgiving each other, just as in Christ God forgave you." – Ephesians 4:32

20.   **Trust in God's Plan:** Pray for unwavering trust in God's plan for your life and assurance that He is guiding you toward a better future.

"For I know the plans I have for you, declares the Lord, plans to prosper you and not to harm you, plans to give you hope and a future." – Jeremiah 29:11

Prayer Points for Healing from Narcissism

1.   **Healing of Emotional Trauma:** Pray for God's healing touch to mend the deep emotional wounds inflicted by narcissistic abuse.

"He heals the brokenhearted and binds up their wounds." – Psalm 147:3

2.   **Restoration of Self-Worth:** Ask for the restoration of your self-worth and identity, affirming that you are valued and loved by God.

"You are precious and honored in My sight, and I love you." – Isaiah 43:4

3.   **Release of Forgiveness:** Seek God's help in releasing any unforgiveness or bitterness toward the narcissist, enabling you to heal fully.

"But if you do not forgive others their sins, your Father will not forgive your sins." – Matthew 6:15

4.   **Renewed Mind:** Pray for the renewal of your mind, freeing you from negative thoughts and patterns instilled by the abuse.

"Do not be conformed to this world, but be transformed by the renewing of your mind." – Romans 12:2

5.   **Peace and Calm:** Ask for peace and calm to replace the anxiety and turmoil caused by the narcissistic relationship.

"Peace I leave with you; My peace I give you. I do not give to you as the world gives." – John 14:27

6.   **Strength to Forgive Yourself:** Request strength and grace to forgive yourself for any perceived mistakes or judgments made during the relationship.

"For if you forgive other people when they sin against you, your heavenly Father will also forgive you." – Matthew 6:14

7. **Restoration of Relationships:** Pray for healing and restoration in relationships that were damaged or strained by narcissistic abuse.

"So then, let us pursue what makes for peace and for mutual upbuilding." – Romans 14:19

8. **Emotional Resilience:** Seek emotional resilience to cope with the ongoing effects of the abuse and to continue healing.

"The Lord is close to the brokenhearted and saves those who are crushed in spirit." – Psalm 34:18

9. **Trust in New Relationships:** Ask God to help you rebuild trust and form healthy relationships moving forward.

"But the fruit of the Spirit is love, joy, peace, forbearance, kindness, goodness, faithfulness, gentleness and self-control." – Galatians 5:22-23

10. **Self-Acceptance:** Pray for the ability to accept and love yourself as you are, without the influence of the narcissist's criticism.

"I praise You because I am fearfully and wonderfully made; Your works are wonderful, I know that full well." – Psalm 139:14

11. **Guidance in Therapy:** Seek God's guidance in finding and engaging with effective therapy or counseling to aid in your healing journey.

"For wisdom will enter your heart, and knowledge will be pleasant to your soul." – Proverbs 2:10

12.   **Protection from Triggers:** Ask for protection and peace from triggers that may cause distress or relapse into old patterns.

"The Lord is a refuge for the oppressed, a stronghold in times of trouble." – Psalm 9:9

13.   **Restoration of Joy:** Pray for the restoration of joy and hope in your life, replacing the emptiness left by the abuse.

"You have turned my mourning into joyful dancing; You have taken away my clothes of mourning and clothed me with joy." – Psalm 30:11

14.   **Divine Comfort:** Seek divine comfort and reassurance in moments of pain and loneliness as you navigate your healing process.

"He comforts us in all our troubles, so that we can comfort those in any trouble, with the comfort we ourselves receive from God." – 2 Corinthians 1:4

15.   **Empowerment to Move Forward:** Ask for empowerment and courage to move forward with your life, embracing new opportunities and experiences.

"I can do all things through Christ who strengthens me." – Philippians 4:13

16.   **Healing of Physical Symptoms:** Pray for healing of any physical symptoms or health issues resulting from the stress of the abuse.

"He took up our pain and bore our suffering, yet we considered Him punished by God, stricken by Him, and afflicted." – Isaiah 53:4

17.   **Gratitude for Growth:** Ask for a grateful heart for the growth and strength gained through the healing process, even amid suffering.

"Give thanks in all circumstances; for this is God's will for you in Christ Jesus." – 1 Thessalonians 5:18

18.   **Guidance for Setting Boundaries:** Seek wisdom in setting healthy boundaries in all relationships to protect your well-being.

"The Lord will guide you always; He will satisfy your needs in a sun-scorched land and will strengthen your frame." – Isaiah 58:11

19.   **Renewed Sense of Purpose:** Pray for a renewed sense of purpose and direction in your life, guided by God's plans for your future.

"Commit to the Lord whatever you do, and He will establish your plans." – Proverbs 16:3

20.   **Joy in God's Presence:** Ask for joy and peace in God's presence, trusting that He is with you every step of the way in your healing journey.

"You make known to me the path of life; You will fill me with joy in Your presence, with eternal pleasures at Your right hand." – Psalm 16:11

Comprehensive Resource List

Here's a comprehensive domestic violence resource list to support survivors and individuals seeking help:

Hotlines

1. **National Domestic Violence Hotline**
   - Phone: 1-800-799-SAFE (7233)
   - Text: START to 88788
   - Website: thehotline.org
   - 24/7 support via phone, text, and online chat for survivors of domestic violence.

2. **National Sexual Assault Hotline (RAINN)**
   - Phone: 1-800-656-HOPE (4673)
   - Website: rainn.org
   - Confidential support and resources for sexual assault survivors.

3. **National Suicide Prevention Lifeline**
   - Phone: 988
   - Website: 988lifeline.org
   - Provides emotional support to individuals in suicidal crisis or emotional distress.

4. **Crisis Text Line**
   - Text: HOME to 741741

- 24/7 emotional support for individuals experiencing a crisis, including domestic violence.

5. **StrongHearts Native Helpline**
   - Phone: 1-844-7NATIVE (1-844-762-8483)
   - Website: strongheartshelpline.org
   - Culturally appropriate support for Native Americans affected by domestic violence.

6. **Veterans Crisis Line**
   - Phone: 988 and press 1
   - Text: 838255
   - Website: veteranscrisisline.net
   - Support for veterans in crisis, including those experiencing domestic violence.

Shelter and Housing Support

1. **The National Coalition Against Domestic Violence (NCADV)**
   - Website: ncadv.org
   - Provides shelter resources and support for survivors of domestic violence.

2. **Women's Law Shelter Directory**
   - Website: womenslaw.org/find-help
   - State-by-state listings of domestic violence shelters and organizations that offer legal assistance.

3. **YWCA USA**
   - Website: ywca.org
   - Provides safe housing, domestic violence shelters, and crisis services for women in need.

4. **Housing and Urban Development (HUD) Domestic Violence Resources**
   - Website: hud.gov

- o Assistance with housing and transitioning to safe homes for survivors of domestic violence.

Legal Resources

1. **WomensLaw.org**
   - o Website: womenslaw.org
   - o Provides legal information and support for survivors of domestic violence, including protection orders.

2. **National Network to End Domestic Violence (NNEDV)**
   - o Website: nnedv.org
   - o Legal advocacy and resources for survivors of domestic violence, including housing, financial aid, and legal guidance.

3. **Legal Aid Society**
   - o Website: legalaid.org
   - o Offers legal representation for survivors, including protection orders, child custody, and divorce.

4. **Family Justice Centers**
   - o Website: familyjusticecenter.org
   - o Provides free legal services, shelter referrals, and support for domestic violence survivors.

Mental Health and Emotional Support

1. **DomesticShelters.org**
   - o Website: domesticshelters.org
   - o A directory of shelters and resources with guides for emotional and mental support.

2. **BetterHelp**
   - o Website: betterhelp.com

- Online counseling with licensed therapists for individuals coping with domestic abuse trauma.

3. **Pandora's Project**

   - Website: pandys.org
   - Support, resources, and forums for survivors of sexual assault and domestic violence.

4. **National Alliance on Mental Illness (NAMI)**

   - Website: nami.org
   - Provides mental health resources and support groups for survivors of domestic violence.

For Men

1. **Domestic Violence Hotline for Men and Women**

   - Phone: 1-888-7HELPLINE (1-888-743-5754)
   - Support services for male victims of domestic violence.

2. **1in6**

   - Website: 1in6.org
   - Support and resources for men who have experienced domestic violence and sexual abuse.

Financial Assistance

1. **The Allstate Foundation: Purple Purse**

   - Website: allstatefoundation.org/purple-purse
   - Financial literacy and economic empowerment for survivors of domestic violence.

2. **The National Domestic Violence Hotline Financial Assistance**

   - Website: thehotline.org
   - Emergency financial assistance for survivors of domestic violence.

3. **FreeFrom**
   - Website: freefrom.org
   - Provides economic justice and resources for survivors of domestic violence to rebuild their financial stability.

This resource list can help individuals in different stages of escaping domestic violence and rebuilding their lives.

About Shannon Savoy

Shannon Savoy is a powerful prophetess, deliverance minister, spiritual warrior, Holy Spirit lead speaker, two-time Amazon best-selling author, mentor, Realtor and founder of Narc Free Living LLC. Located in Houston, TX, Narc Free Living is a Kingdom-building ministry and Kingdom business that is committed to dismantling and disrupting narcissistic & demonic systems by the Blood of Jesus and God's word. Shannon leads corporate training, prayer & fasting, workshops for survivors, YouTube teachings, one-on-one & group coaching - all designed to turn victims into women of warfare.

Shannon is a certified trauma-informed, Introspective Life & Narcissist Abuse Recovery Coach. She is a forward-thinking transformative leader & a decorated Army Veteran of 23 years. She retired in 2017, achieving the rank of Chief Warrant Officer Four. As a survivor of domestic interpersonal violence, she is an advocate against abuse and was awarded Voice of the Voiceless in 2021. Shannon equips, edifies, exhorts, and empowers others to break the chains of abuse. She formed Chain Breaker University (CBU) to help transform voiceless victims into well-trained women of warfare. CBU helps Chain Breakers walk into their God-given purpose by addressing & breaking generational curses, chains, and cycles. Shannon holds an undergraduate degree in Information Technology Management with an emphasis in Project Management.

Narc Free Living® is a ministry and coaching brand that is committed to dismantling, disrupting narcissistic & demonic systems through Holy-Spirit lead exhortations, edification, education, the Blood of Jesus, and God's word. Visit NarcFreeLiving.com and follow @narcfreelivingllc on YouTube, Instagram, TikTok, and Facebook for in-depth teachings. Let's break those chains!

www.narcfreeliving.com

Made in the USA
Las Vegas, NV
24 October 2024